Here is what reviewers and readers are saying about *Pet Sitting for Profit:*

". . . this book is an absolute must. It covers everything from office procedures, legal structure, telephone techniques and customer complaints to contracts and advertising."

—*DOG WEEK*

"We highly recommend this . . . a must for anybody interested in taking up pet sitting as a business or as a sideline."

—*CATS Magazine*

"Moran deals with the basics of starting your own pet sitting business. The book covers all aspects of starting a home-based business . . . "

—*Aiken Standard*

" '. . . good things come in small packages' will be proven for those who read Patti Moran's timely treatise: *Pet Sitting for Profit.* The book holds an opportunity for all pet lovers, for those who wish to be their own boss on a full time basis, those who want or need the income of a second job, as well as those retired and desirous of meaningful activity."

—*The Latham Letter*

"Running a pet sitting business is more complicated than it sounds, and Moran provides a wealth of detail about how the business should be handled. . . . The book is certainly a handy guide for anyone considering such a business, but it also contains helpful information for people who need pet-sitters."

—*CAT FANCY*

"This is the book for the person who thinks that they might like the work and the responsibility of this type of business. The book includes everything you need to know about setting up the business."

—*Rainbo Electronic Reviews*

"The book is great. It certainly will take all the guesswork out of setting up a pet-sitting business!"

—Elizabeth Nicholson
Richton Park, Illinois

PET SITTING FOR PROFIT

PET SITTING FOR PROFIT

A Complete Manual for Professional Success

Patti J. Moran

Howell Book House
New York

Illustrations by Robert Youngquist and Michelle Boles

Copyright © 1987, 1991, 1997 by Patti J. Moran

Howell Book House
A Simon & Schuster Macmillan Company
1633 Broadway
New York, NY 10019

MACMILLAN is a registered trademark of Macmillan, Inc.

Library of Congress Cataloging-in-Publication Data

Moran, Patti J.
    Pet sitting for profit : a complete manual for professional
success / Patti J. Moran.
        p.   cm.
    ISBN 0-87605-596-X
    1. Pet sitting—Handbooks, manuals, etc.   2. New business
enterprises—Handbooks, manuals, etc.   I. Title.
    SF414.34.M67   1997
    636.088'7—dc21   97-27615
                                                      CIP

Manufactured in the United States of America

10 9 8 7 6 5 4

Book design by Rachael McBrearty, Madhouse Productions

For my three angels, Lonnie, Lucy, and Ennis. And for Mike, whose love and support has made it all possible—and one heck of an adventure.

With special thanks to dear Dotty—who shares my passion for pet sitting. And to the many wonderful pet sitters I've met along the way—whose dedication, commitment and professionalism make me so proud—and whose friendship I will always cherish.

CONTENTS

Introduction xiii

1. THE CONCEPT OF PET SITTING _____ 1
Factors Contributing to Success
Trends Contributing to the Growth of the Industry
So How Many Pets Did You Say Are out There?
Advantages of Operating a Pet-Sitting Service
How Much Can I Make?
Pet Sitting versus Other Small Businesses
The Alternatives to Pet Sitting
The Need Is Everywhere

2. GETTING STARTED _____ 12
Research and Resources
Pet Sitters International (PSI)
Marketing Survey
Naming Your Business
Business Logo
Business License
Office Location
Legal Structure
Finding an Accountant
Selecting a Bank
Insurance
Dishonesty Bond
Basic Office Supplies and Furnishings
Business Telephone

3. OFFICE PROCEDURES _____ 38

Customer Card System
Sitter Schedule Sheets
Handling Delinquent Accounts
Small Claims Court
More Account Collection Tips
Policies and Procedures
Telephone Techniques
Answering Machines versus Personal Answering Services
Pagers and Cellular Phones
Determining Service Routes
Setting Prices
Holiday Fees
Compensating Sitters
Handling Customer Complaints
"Always Ready" Service
Planning for Disasters
Client Interviews and Client Presentation Books
Using a Computer

4. PERSONNEL _____ 72

Finding and Qualifying Pet Sitters
Applicant Interviews
Sitter Orientation
Sitter Safety
Sitter Nutrition
Survival Items
Managing and Motivating Sitters
Staff Meetings
Employees versus Independent Contractors

5. ADVERTISING _____ 105

The Means to the Masses
The Importance of a Brochure
A Word About "Licensing"
Brochure and Business Card Uses

Inexpensive Ways to Advertise
Reaching the Masses—That Is the Question
Newspapers
Yellow Pages
Television
Radio
The Familiar Image
More Great Advertising Ideas from Readers

6. PUBLIC RELATIONS _____ **141**
Developing a Newsletter
News Releases
Public Speaking
Exhibition Booths
Special Events
Business Etiquette

7. EXAMINING THE NEGATIVES _____ **153**
Just Say No
Other Possible Problems and How to Handle or Avoid Them
The Best from the Best—Tips from the Field

8. USEFUL BUSINESS FORMS _____ **173**
Designing a Service Contract
Daily Log
Evaluation Form
Client Reservation Form
Notification Forms
Additional Forms
Tips from Pet Sitters

9. CLOSING YOUR BUSINESS _____ **187**
How a Business Broker Can Assist
Ps and Qs of Saying Good-bye

10. IN CONCLUSION _____ **191**

Tracking Your Growth
Business Trends
Crime Deterrence
Overnight Pet and House Sitting
Expanded Services
Some Closing Thoughts

ADDENDA _____ **195**

Estimated Start-Up Costs and Checklist
Helpful Products for Professional Pet Sitters
Pet-Related Organizations
PSI Recommendations for Excellence in Pet Sitting
Postscript

Introduction

No one knows what he can do till he tries.

—Publilius Syrus, Maxim 786

Whatever you think you can do, or dream you can do, begin it.
Boldness has genius, magic and power in it.

—Goethe

If at once you have begun, never leave it till it's done. Be it big or be it small, do it well or not at all.

—My mother

The word has gotten out. Americans are crazy about their pets. A recent survey, conducted by The American Animal Hospital Association, of 1,019 pet owners in the United States and Canada found that:

80% give their pets holiday or birthday gifts

77% regard themselves as parents or guardians of their pets

54% would prefer their pet's company to that of a human if trapped on a deserted island

48% prepare special meals for their pets

33% call home to talk to their pets through telephone answering machines

Another study, by The HomeCare Council, lends further proof to the importance of today's pets to their owners:

88% said they would risk injury or death to save their pets' lives

66% strongly agreed that their pets were like children to them

44% allow their pets to sleep with them in their beds

22% feel closer to their pets than to their spouses

And, a Gallup Poll that appeared in the December 24, 1990 issue of *U.S. News & World Report* stated:

9 out of 10 pet owners talk to their pets

30% leave the television on for their pets

17% keep their pets' photo in their wallet

Finally! Here is statistical data to substantiate what I, as a professional pet sitter, have known for years: There is a new attitude towards pets in today's society. American pet owners do think of their pets as surrogate children—and they are willing to pamper and treat their pets as if they are children.

This new attitude—and public recognition of the role of pets in today's society—has led to the understanding and acceptance of a new term in America's pet-owning households: *pet sitter.*

When I reflect upon the years since 1983, the year I started my pet-sitting business, it's almost overwhelming to consider the changes and growth the pet-sitting field has experienced, and to consider how pet sitting has affected me personally and professionally. Little did I know in 1983 that opening a small, part-time pet-sitting service would lead me not only to author this book, but also to help bring the professional pet-sitting industry into one of prominence, credibility, and respectability.

While some people and some communities still are not familiar with the at-home pet care services provided by professional pet sitters, the industry has truly come a long way. It is a changed—and much more receptive—world to pet sitting, much different from what I experienced back in 1983! Today's pet sitter does not have to endure the laughs from skeptics who say in disbelief, "You do what?!" (Well, there probably will always be a few you'll have to tolerate. . . .) Nor does today's pet sitter have to spend hours looking for good business liability coverage— a tailor-made policy exists for our burgeoning industry.

No longer is trial and error a mandatory part of the learning process for today's pet-sitting professional. Tried and true procedures, methods and tips are readily available in such publications as this, along with other numerous resources, such as professional organizations and products that specifically target pet sitters.

Although today's pet sitter will make some mistakes (no matter how many times I advise you to always test a client's house key, you still will have to find yourself locked out of a house before you make it a practice of doing this) there's really not a whole lot of excuses available if you've done your homework. If you're seriously considering professional pet sitting as a career, the best homework assignment I can give you is to read this book in full. In this book, I've compiled the best—and the worst—of my experiences in pet sitting. I include a lot of hard-won lessons and exper-tise—not only from me, but from many of my colleagues as well.

Having the opportunity to author this book, as well as to found two pet-sitting associations (national and international), has put me in direct contact with many other professionals in the field. We all have learned and grown professionally from this contact and communication—many of us have become good friends in the process. Since selling my pet-sitting business in 1993 to devote more time to promoting professional pet sitting, much of my pet sitting has been done vicariously—through the eyes, ears and experiences of colleagues who actively pet sit. My initial requests from eccentric pet owners who wanted a special meal prepared or game played with their pet now seem tame compared to the stories related to me by colleagues! Never was I asked to actually drive a dog around the block (talk about pampered) or sing show tunes to a parrot or care for a pet lobster originally intended as an edible gift. . . . But, thanks to my colleagues, pet sitting still remains fascinating and fun even from my desk, and I continue to learn, grow and enjoy this adventure in pet sitting.

In all of my years in pet sitting, something that has become increasingly clear is that there is no one way to run a pet-sitting service. Because each pet, customer, home and assignment is different, there is no "one size fits all" when it comes to pet sitting. You will be wise to read and learn as much as possible about this career so that you can make the right choices in pet sitting.

Due to the ever-changing, evolving world of pet sitting, I'm convinced that no one can know it all or have all the answers. Although some flatter me by saying I'm the wise old sage of pet sitting, I'll be the first to tell you that I don't begin to know it all! What I do know is that people attracted to this career seem to be the nicest people who care about being their professional best. And by sharing experiences, we can learn and improve and grow together. And now, read on.

■

A friend recently asked why I was spending so much time revising and expanding this book when the preceding editions have sold so well. Several reasons immediately came to mind.

First, in anything I do, I like to do it well (thanks in large part to my dear, late mother, who is quoted in the Introduction to this book). This philosophy was evident in the first editions of *Pet Sitting for Profit*, and I believe my thoroughness is what has earned my book its reputation as the "bible of pet sitting."

With such high praise from thousands of readers, I unknowingly created equally high expectations for subsequent editions!

Second, as I previously mentioned, the pet-sitting industry continues to evolve. In each revision, I have attempted to address the trends that were taking place within the industry and the relevant issues. For example, the critical need for good (but often difficult to obtain) business liability insurance was stressed in earlier editions. Thanks to the proliferation of pet sitters in recent years, this need has been recognized by the insurance industry and an excellent policy has been made available. However, with the increase in pet-sitting services, subsequent editions stressed the need to protect the name of your business. When there were only a handful of pet sitters, name recognition and protection weren't given a second thought. In earlier revisions, I stressed the importance of giving careful consideration to this facet of starting and running a business. Similarly, in this revision I will attempt to keep you on the "cutting edge" of what is happening in professional pet sitting.

A third motivation has come from you, the reader. Many of you have written to ask me questions, solicit advice or share your own experiences in starting and operating your pet-sitting businesses. Although I have not been able to reply personally in all cases, I have read and appreciated your communication. It's through your communication that I've noted mutual concerns and areas needing more attention in revised editions of *Pet Sitting for Profit*. I thank you for letting me know how I can improve this book and better help the pet sitters of tomorrow. I sincerely hope this new edition meets the high standards you've come to expect from me.

■

Many readers have been curious about my background, how I came up with the idea of pet sitting and how I came to write a book about the subject. Others have asked if I intentionally set out to create an industry. So, for those who are interested in such things, I offer the following.

It all started in 1983 when I was laid off from my job. Actually, management positions are terminated (versus laid off) when companies undergo downsizing—whatever you want to call it, I found myself unemployed. If anyone had told me then that losing my job was a blessing in disguise, I wouldn't have believed them. I had been hired by a large manufacturing company one week after graduating from college. I spent seven years there in employee relations, working my way up from a clerical position to management. My position was stress-filled due to the workload and company politics. The salary and benefits, however, were generous, and somehow, I resigned myself to the fact that it was easier to stay than to leave. When the company experienced a severe downturn in business, almost half of the employees, including myself, found themselves without a job.

Because I needed the income, I found myself exploring job options. The idea of having my own business had always appealed to me, and at that point, it was more attractive than ever. The thought of not having to answer to anyone else or depend upon anyone else for job security encouraged me to seriously consider starting my own business. My biggest question was what kind of business to open.

As I slowly researched various ideas, I also took time out for myself. I planted a garden. I took classes. I mowed the grass on cool weekday mornings. I shopped during the day when there was hardly anyone in the stores. These activities were all luxuries to me after seven years in the corporate rat race, years when time was limited and dictated by the demands of my job. I rapidly became spoiled by my flexible schedule, and the idea of an eight-to-five office job actually grew abhorrent. What could I do that would provide adequate income and allow me time to enjoy this newfound and treasured lifestyle?

The answer came when a good friend who'd recently moved to another city visited for a weekend. Knowing how crazy she was about her dog, I inquired about what type of arrangements she had made for her pet's care during her absence. She told me she had hired a pet sitter to come to her house twice a day. Little did I know then that this innocent question and her answer would change my life as I knew it . . . but it was then and there that the light bulb went on in my head. I was immediately intrigued.

Having three dogs and a cat of my own at the time, I was all too familiar with the problems a pet owner faces when traveling. I knew firsthand that the option of a pet-sitting service would be a needed and welcome one in my community. Furthermore, pet sitting could be done in just a few hours in the morning and in the late afternoon, so I'd have some flexibility and extra hours in my day for other activities. It wouldn't require a costly inventory, and I certainly wouldn't need an expensive wardrobe. I also didn't see any need for renting office space initially; pet sitting seemed to me to be an ideal choice for a home business. And because I loved animals, pet sitting would allow me to get paid for doing something I enjoyed. It quickly became apparent to me that a pet-sitting business had many advantages and incorporated all the things I was looking for in a new career venture. Although it was scary to consider the risk I'd be taking in opening an "unheard of" business in our town, I felt I should at least give it a try.

As I made preparations to open my pet-sitting service, there were times when I thought I might be crazy. First, although there was a lot of information available about how to start a small business, I couldn't find any information that specifically addressed pet sitting. Second, I was often not taken seriously when I told people what I was attempting to do. Some of my friends just couldn't believe I planned to "baby-sit for pets and clean litter boxes for a living." And, as I searched for business insurance coverage, many doors were shut in my face.

But, as the saying goes, where there's a will, there's a way. In late 1983, my pet-sitting service opened for business. Since that time, this relatively new and innovative business has provided me with a very rewarding, interesting and profitable career.

I originally was prompted to write this book for a couple of reasons. As people in other parts of the country heard about my business, I began receiving requests for help and information from budding entrepreneurs who wanted to start such a business in their own area. Because there was nothing available in writing to help me when I first started pet sitting, I knew firsthand the need for such guidance. I also wrote the book (and initially published it myself) because I believed that pet sitting is a viable new profession. It provides a valuable service for pets and their owners and an enjoyable and profitable way for pet lovers to earn a livelihood.

In writing the book to help others get started more easily, did I set out to create an industry? No, one step just naturally led to another—with several steps being suggested by readers and colleagues along the way. This book and the information it contains launched others into the career. With the proliferation came the request for products and items that would be useful to professional pet sitters (and thus launched my products company, Patti Moran's), and the need for an organization to unite pet sitters soon followed. While I half-kiddingly say it's good that I didn't know what I was getting into (ignorance is bliss!) and all the work I was creating for myself with my passion for pet sitting, I am very grateful for the accolades afforded my efforts. I have worked hard to advance the profession of pet sitting and, being only human, find it's nice and gratifying to have my endeavors recognized and appreciated.

Do I still own and operate a pet-sitting business? No, it was with some sadness—and a lot of pride—that I sold my ten-year-old service in November, 1993. I had not done any "hands-on" pet sitting (the fun part of the business!) in almost seven years, because managing the business had become almost a full-time job. Trying to run it, along with a pet-sitting association and a pet-sitting products company had become a bit much. So, when an offer came along that I couldn't refuse, I did sell my local service so I could concentrate my time and energies towards growing, improving and supporting professional pet sitting on a larger scale. To an extent, selling the business was like letting go of a child. It was something I had lovingly and carefully nurtured and built. At the same time, it was exhilarating to build a business that had value and was salable! And with selling my business, a new milestone in pet sitting was reached. No longer was pet sitting a business to be "laughed at"; instead it had become an established, profitable business to buy!

Being at the forefront of the industry, I have seen it grow from only a handful of us back in 1983 to an estimated 2,500 companies in the U.S. today. Even with this phenomenal growth, I firmly believe that this field is still in its infancy. I see parallels between pet sitting and pizza—if you'll indulge me for just a minute.

I remember, as a kid growing up in the sixties, how pizza—while certainly not a new dish in food history—experienced what can be described as a food revolution! In our home it was something different for dinner and really quite a treat. However, the only way to have a pizza back then was to make it from scratch or from a mix. Then came the 1970s with pizzerias and pizza restaurant chains making their way across the country. The love affair with pizza continued into the 1980s with home deliveries of pizza, numerous pizza chains, and all sorts of frozen varieties and ready-made crusts widely available in stores. Today pizza is still big business; there's a pizza shop (or two!) in every community. Pizza has become a household staple!

Professional pet sitting is going through a similar evolution. It was a fairly new concept during the 1980s, but as the pet-owning consumer's awareness has grown about the advantages of in-home pet care, so has the demand for in-home care. Although there isn't a pet sitter on every block in America yet, pet sitters are starting to specialize in cat care or bird care or horse care. The progress has come in the acceptance—and a warm one at that—of the public's perception and use of professional pet sitters. In the 1990s, having a pet sitter is as natural as ordering a pizza!

There are a couple of reasons I think pet sitting offers tremendous career opportunities and is nowhere near the size of the industry it will become. One is that it lends itself beautifully to being a small, home-based business. I've heard from countless "stay-at-home" moms (and a few dads!) who were delighted to hear that professional pet sitting had become a credible occupation. "I was doing this anyway for everyone in the neighborhood," they've told me—they're now turning these time-consuming neighborhood favors into small, income-producing business ventures! But that's the great thing about pet sitting—it can be done on a small scale in a neighborhood subdivision or condominium complex—or it can be done on a large scale with a staff of pet sitters covering a wide city/county area. One thing is for sure—pets are everywhere. In subdivisions, apartment complexes, rural farms—and they all need conscientious daily care.

How many pets are there? According to the 1994 National Pet Owners Survey conducted by the American Pet Products Manufacturers Association (APPMA), there are almost 270,000,000 pets projected in the six major animal categories alone (dog, cat, reptile, bird, fish, small animal), which translates to pets outnumbering people in the U.S.!

Based on a survey of the members of Pet Sitters International in 1995, pet sitters, while earning an estimated 35 million of the $20 billion spent annually on pets, still serve less than 1% of the pet-owning public. This is the second reason I believe pet sitting has tremendous career potential—there is a lot more business out there to be garnered by existing—and new—pet sitters.

Before you get all dizzy-headed from dollar signs in your eyes, let me point out that there is a lot more to pet sitting than meets the eye. It's not, as some would think, a fast way to make a buck. Hanging a shingle out and calling yourself a pet sitter is not enough to be successful in today's business world. Having a love of animals is not even enough to assure you success in pet sitting. All too often I've heard of pet sitters who get into this business thinking that their love and enjoyment of animals will sustain them. Then, three or four months down the road they're out of business. These "fly by nights" reflect poorly upon the industry. Therefore, I urge you, as a prospective entrepreneur, to give this promising and unique venture your careful consideration. Consider all the angles and the necessary ingredients to running a successful pet-sitting service—above all keeping in mind that it is a business. Careful forethought will assure that your journey into pet sitting will be a successful and satisfying venture.

CHAPTER 1

THE CONCEPT OF PET SITTING

For all the strides we've made in professional pet sitting, as of this writing, you still will not find the word defined in any dictionary. Although pet sitters have become important players in the pet-care arena and "pet sitter" is a household term, we still aren't recognized in the household dictionary! (At Pet Sitters International, we have launched a "dictionary campaign," so hopefully this will change very soon!)

For now, readers will have to settle for a definition of pet sitting "according to Patti," which in its simplest and purest form reads:

> *Pet sitter*—a person hired to take care of another's pet (or pets), usually in the pet's home environment.

The key words in this "purest" definition are "in the pet's home environment." To me, this unique concept has played a major role in the popularity of our services. We go to the pet—allowing it to stay in its comfortable and secure surroundings. I know that some professed pet sitters have included in their range of services placing the pet in the home of another caretaker or even bringing the pet into the sitter's own home. To me, this is not pet sitting in its truest sense. Mid-day dog walking does qualify as pet sitting, though, because the dog walker is actually going to the pet's home to give the pet a daily dose of exercise and TLC. I realize that some pets do fine as a visitor in another household; however, this arrangement is closer to boarding than to pet sitting.

Although the concept of pet sitting is much more widely known now than it was in the 1980s, I constantly hear from someone who has just "discovered" the wonderful world of at-home pet care. In some instances, these calls are from pet owners who want to find a good pet sitter, and others are from intrigued "wannabe pet sitters." This tells me that even though pet sitting has come a long way, we still have much to do in the way of educating the general public. The United States is a huge country with many animal lovers who indeed may not have heard of this relatively new industry and thus may never have considered pet sitting as a profitable business venture.

FACTORS CONTRIBUTING TO SUCCESS

Whether you have just learned of this industry or have been aware of it for some time, I urge you to consider the potential a pet-sitting business can hold—potential for self-employment, for providing a needed community service, for creating the lifestyle you've always dreamed of and for significant profits.

By starting a pet-sitting service, you'll enter the service industry, which is expected to be a powerful economic force of the future. Experts say that people today need services of all sorts. Statistics show that in the United States, services now account for nearly 70 percent of the Gross National Product. Twenty-two million of the 25 million jobs created since 1970 were in the service sector. According to the Bureau of Labor Statistics, the number of "animal caretakers," a category that includes pet walkers, is expected to grow 38 percent between 1990 and 2005.

These figures are very encouraging to anyone thinking of starting a pet-sitting service. With your own pet-sitting business, you'll join the fast track of the new, service-oriented American economy.

If you're a female contemplating getting into pet sitting, you'll be further encouraged to know that the National Foundation for Women Business Owners reports that there are now 7.95 million companies owned by women, up from 4.48 million in 1987. This 78-percent growth dwarfs the 47-percent growth for all firms in the United States.

The 1995 membership of Pet Sitters International (PSI), an educational organization for professional pet sitters, was 91 percent female.

Although more and more men are getting into this career, pet sitting has been a female-dominated industry to date. Perhaps it naturally attracts females because of the nurturing involved in caring for animals (nurturing has traditionally been associated with women). Whatever the reason, I'm proud that pet sitting has provided a way for many women to enjoy the rewards, personally and professionally, of entrepreneurship. But I am glad to see many men recognizing that pet sitting is a viable and profitable business venture!

Trends Contributing to the Growth of the Industry

The following trends in today's society have made service businesses—and pet sitting—fast-growing industries:

- Two-income families have become the norm, making services both needed and affordable to these families. Travel for pleasure also is more affordable, which increases the likelihood that pet care will be needed during such absences from home.

- Young professionals delay marriage and/or children; many are owning pets and taking better care of them than ever before.

- The same is true of "empty nesters," who are getting pets and treating them as surrogate children.

  > Note: The "yuppies" of the 80s have been replaced in the 90s with the "dinks" (dual income, no kids) and "dips" (dual income, pets)! The "dips" comprise a profitable market for pet sitters!

Another trend in American society is the move toward self-employment, often in a home-based setting. More and more of us are discovering that our jobs rule our lives, and contrary to generations past, we're finding in today's world that there is no such thing as job security. Self-employment allows you to take control of your life, your career, your schedule, and your income. As a pet sitter, you are your own boss. You decide when you work, where you work, what you charge and for whom you work. There is no one looking over your shoulder and no time clock to punch.

Perhaps due to the downsizing in corporate America, we have become a transient society. People come and go, often not staying in a place long enough to get to know their neighbors. And, even if you do know your neighbors, that doesn't mean you want them in your home when you're away or that you feel comfortable requesting pet-care services from them.

Another trend in today's society that has given rise to service industries is that we're a busy society! Geez, how did we get so busy? Never have we had so many conveniences to make life easier, yet it seems we never have enough time to get it all done. Enter house cleaners, lawn services, car detailers and yes, pet sitters. Convenience has become the name of the game. (Oh, and let's not forget those pizza delivery personnel either!)

A negative trend that has enhanced the popularity of at-home pet care is the prevalence of crime. We see and hear about crime on an almost daily basis through the media; unfortunately, no one and no community is immune from it. However, there is a great deal of public concern about crime. People love the fact that by using a professional pet sitter, their home is being checked on at the same time that their pets are being cared for. While making pet-care visits, pet sitters provide a measure of crime-deterrence because they make the home appear inhabited. This feature in itself is a real selling point for our service.

Last, but certainly not least, is the trend in America to anthropomorphize our pets. And here, for a definition, we can turn to the dictionary: Anthropomorphism is defined as "the attributing of human shape or characteristics to a god, animal, or inanimate thing." This tendency has elevated the pet to a full-fledged family member, a surrogate child—the all-important companion who has needs, feelings, thoughts and personality traits. We talk to them, pamper them and want only the best for our "babies." The best includes a pet sitter!

SO HOW MANY PETS DID YOU SAY ARE OUT THERE?

Figures released from the 1994 American Pet Products Manufacturers Association Pet Ownership Survey indicated the following trends in the United States' pet population:

Cats: 65 million in over 30 million households

Dogs: 57 million in 35 million households

Freshwater and marine fish: 100 million in 11 million households

Birds: 15 million in almost 6 million households

Small Animals: 12 million in almost 5 million households
(32 percent rabbits, 26 percent hamsters, 13 percent guinea pigs,
9 percent mice or rats, 6 percent gerbils, 2 percent potbellied pigs,
2 percent chinchillas)

Reptiles: 7 million in almost 3 million households (38 percent
turtles or tortoises, 25 percent iguanas, 19 percent snakes,
10 percent lizards, 8 percent frogs or toads)

Figures were not available from this survey for the number of ferrets or hermit crabs kept as pets; however, these animals are found in many pet-owning households. Livestock figures also were not available, although at-home care of horses, cows, goats, pigs, sheep and even ducks and chickens can be an important and profitable business for professional pet sitters.

ADVANTAGES OF OPERATING A PET-SITTING SERVICE

If you've always dreamed of owning your own business, it is true that there is an exhilarating independence and pride that comes in being your own boss. An added bonus is that becoming a business owner will give you an increased sense of self-worth and confidence in your abilities. I've had letters from many stay-at-home mothers who found that their pet-sitting services helped them rebuild their work skills and confidence levels while contributing to the family income at the same time. I've heard from retirees who said their pet-sitting services allowed them to remain active and to feel like contributing members of society. The self-satisfaction you'll derive is only one of the many benefits you'll experience as the owner of your own pet-sitting service. Although you may work longer hours, work usually becomes more enjoyable when you're working for yourself.

Being a pet sitter gives you flexibility with your daily schedule. You'll no longer be bound by a rigid eight-to-five work routine. Because most pet-sitting visits are made during the early morning or early evening hours, you'll have the largest part of the day free to pursue other interests or even to work another job. The flexible working hours make pet sitting an ideal part-time business or second income for many people because pet-sitting responsibilities can be adapted to most schedules. And, of course it can be operated as a full-time business in many cities.

Becoming a pet sitter will provide a means of income. Whether you sit independently or employ a staff of sitters, there is money to be made by providing this valuable service to your community.

HOW MUCH CAN I MAKE?

The amount of income you can expect to make will depend on several variables. The location of a pet-sitting service is a factor in income potential. A heavily populated city area will naturally provide a greater number of customers than a rural setting. A part-time sitting service will not generate as much income as a full-time service. And a pet sitter working alone will not generate as much revenue as would a staff of busy pet sitters.

Another important ingredient to the income expectations of a pet-sitting service is the personality of the owner of the business. A business owner who does nothing but print up some business cards and sit by the phone will find himself only dreaming of income. A business owner who commits himself to the success of his business and then actively and aggressively pursues this commitment has a better chance of realizing high income expectations.

The chapters that follow on advertising and public relations will provide you with excellent ways to assertively and aggressively promote your pet-sitting business; however, it is up to you to follow through with the implementation.

Although pet sitting is a terrific business idea, it takes more than a good idea to make a business a success. I'm often asked by readers "how much can I expect to make?"—this is one question I can't answer. I don't know the reader's capabilities, desires and level of commitment.

I can give you some information that will help you to make your own income projections when assessing pet sitting as a career. Two national surveys of pet sitters have indicated that the national average for a pet-sitting visit is approximately $12.00. Using this national average, you can determine the number of pet-sitting visits you anticipate making on a daily, weekly, monthly and yearly basis. (If you plan to utilize a staff of pet sitters, you'll need to project their visits as well.) You then multiply this number by the average charge of $12.00 per visit to estimate your gross annual revenues. Of course, you'll need to estimate expenses that will be paid from your gross revenues to determine the income you will net, but this formula will give you a means of making income projections. After estimating your daily visits for the yearly income you want to make, you'll need to set your marketing goals for how to achieve this level of business. I will discuss several marketing and advertising techniques that will build your business (and revenues) in Chapters 5 and 6.

Although I can't tell you with any certainty what you, personally, can expect to earn through pet sitting, I can tell you that pet sitting has been profitable for me. My experience has shown that pet owners do not mind paying for peace of mind when they have to be away from home. I also can provide you with information and tools that will get you headed in the right direction for success!

PET SITTING VERSUS OTHER SMALL BUSINESSES

Opportunities

Unlike many other business opportunities, pet sitting involves limited start-up costs. As of this writing, I estimate that a professional pet-sitting service can be opened with a $3,000–$5,000 investment, depending on the cost of living in various parts of the country. (If you plan to pet sit on a small scale just for additional or secondary income, your start-up costs can be much less.)

Although you can spend a lot more, it really isn't necessary. After all, there is no costly inventory required, so your primary expenses will be for liability insurance, a dishonesty bond, office equipment, supplies and professional services. And because pet sitting is an ideal home-based business, you can save money by not having to rent office space. The details of how to open a pet-sitting service economically will be discussed in later chapters.

Presently, pet sitting requires very little in the way of past experience or expertise. This may change in the near future though, due to accreditation and certification programs that are becoming available through national trade organizations. As the number of professional pet sitters increases, the additional education and training afforded by such programs may become a distinguishing factor and competitive edge among industry members. As of this writing, these programs are strictly voluntary and there are no specific educational background requirements for pet sitters. However, any background in working with or caring for pets (even on a personal basis) will be a plus. In addition, any prior business courses or business experience are bound to be helpful in operating your business. I would say that the most important prerequisite of a pet sitter is that he or she needs to be a pet lover. Besides this, possessing good common sense, being responsible, reliable, honest, trustworthy and having a sense of humor are the essential qualities needed for pet sitting.

Another important thing that pet sitting has going for it is that work becomes fun! Many sitters have said to me that pet sitting is so enjoyable that they almost don't feel like they're working. Each pet, home and customer is different, adding variety and interest to the job. Pets and their owners are so appreciative of your efforts, and the pets readily let you know it. Perhaps you have worked for that boss or supervisor whose praise, compliments or positive "strokes" were few and far between—not so with pet sitting. That wagging tail or contented purring lets you know someone is glad you're there. And furthermore, pets don't care what you're wearing or how you look. It's a wonderful feeling to wake up on a rainy morning, throw on jeans and a sweatshirt and head out the door to destinations where you'll be eagerly and warmly greeted.

You'll also take pride in knowing you're providing such a valuable service to your community. Pet owners have had few choices in the past. Traditionally, they could either leave their pets in unfamiliar environments, impose upon a friend or neighbor or stay at home. By opening a pet-sitting service, you're providing a preferred alternative for pet owners, thus enabling them to travel with the assurance that their pets and home are in good hands.

THE ALTERNATIVES TO PET SITTING

Let's discuss the traditional choices a pet owner has had in the past and why personalized home pet care has become such a popular alternative.

When faced with traveling, a pet owner usually has called upon a kennel or veterinarian to board his or her pet. Although some pets do very well in a kennel environment and look forward to it as "camp," many other pets find a strange environment filled with other strange animals to be an upsetting experience. Many pet owners have told me they have had a vacation spoiled by the memory of those sad and confused eyes they left behind. Some said they even had to tranquilize their pets to transport them to boarding facilities. Older pets, especially, are traumatized by a change in environment. By calling on the services of a pet sitter, the owner can leave the pet in its own secure, familiar space. Pets are creatures of habit, just as people are; by staying in their own home they are able to follow their normal eating, medication and exercise routines. Such familiarity contributes to the happiness and healthiness of the pet. Plus, it eliminates the pet owners' need to worry about the welfare of their pet(s).

When using a pet sitter, the owner is not inconvenienced by having to transport his or her pet to the vet or kennel, nor is there the trauma of traveling for the pet. An additional benefit of staying at home is that the likelihood of exposure to illnesses is greatly reduced for the pet. Perhaps most important, a pet receives loving, individual attention from his or her personal pet sitter.

Another option pet owners have is to call upon a friend or neighborhood kid to care for their pets when they must be away. In today's transient society, many people don't know their neighbors well enough to feel comfortable in making this request or just don't want to impose on a friend. What if the neighborhood kid brings in half the neighborhood with him? What if something should happen and the pet becomes ill or something in the house gets broken? Such circumstances could certainly strain or ruin a friendship. There is security in calling a professionally operated pet-sitting service that employs sitters who are accustomed to transporting an ill pet to the vet and who also are insured for breakage in a customer's home. A professional pet-sitting service has reliable, responsible, mature, trustworthy individuals who enjoy the business of caring for pets. A pet sitter can be counted on to treat each pet and home as if it were her own.

There are additional benefits to the pet owner when engaging the services of a pet sitter. A pet sitter keeps an eye on each home by doing such things as bringing in the mail and newspapers, alternating lights, opening and closing curtains or blinds and watering house plants. These small services give a home a "lived in" look while the owner is away. Such crime-deterring measures result in additional peace of mind for the absent homeowner. It is a pleasure for returning homeowners to find healthy and happy pets awaiting their arrival—and their home as they left it.

A pet sitter is also "only a phone call away." Who hasn't left on vacation and thirty miles away from home wondered, "did I turn off the coffee pot (or iron or electric rollers)?" A phone call to the pet sitter can result in an extra visit to the home that will alleviate this nagging worry for the customer!

Expense may be the only negative for a pet owner who engages the services of a pet sitter. A pet sitter is usually a bit more expensive than a kennel (unless it's a multiple pet household—then using a pet sitter is usually less expensive than a kennel) or neighbor. But the number of repeat clients I had and the feedback I got from them attests to the fact that most pet owners think the convenience and advantages afforded by a pet sitter are well worth a little extra expense.

THE NEED IS EVERYWHERE

One of the most positive factors to consider when evaluating pet sitting as a possible business is that virtually every community, urban and rural, really needs such a service. Where there are people, there are pets.

Recent research has identified the therapeutic effect pets have on people. Pets help reduce blood pressure, provide purpose, and combat loneliness. And with crime on the rise in many areas, many dogs are finding homes because of the crime-deterrence they provide. Given these incentives for having a pet, the shrinking size of the American family, the increasing numbers of older people and unmarried adults living alone, it is safe to assume that pet ownership will continue to grow.

To determine if the need for a pet-sitting service exists in your area, check the local Yellow Pages for listings or call veterinarians, groomers and pet stores to see if any such business exists in your community. If you live in a rural area, remember that farmers and livestock owners often have a difficult time leaving home, so your service could be a real godsend. If there is already a service operating and you don't live in a sparsely populated area, there's probably room for more than one pet-sitting business.

Convinced that this business is for you? If so, the rest of this book is written to walk you through opening a professional and reputable pet-sitting service. I suggest you read through it for a general overview of what the profession entails; then, go back and concentrate on specific chapters as you proceed with your own pet-sitting business. If you're already pet sitting professionally, there is much information in this book that may give you ideas on how to improve your existing business. At the risk of sounding like a broken record, oh what I would have given to have had this book available to me when I was starting and operating my pet-sitting business!

CHAPTER 2

GETTING STARTED

RESEARCH AND RESOURCES

Today's new entrepreneur has a wealth of information and resources available that will assist and explain how to start a small business. It's important to spend time seeking out these resources so that you can learn as much as possible before opening your pet-sitting service. I firmly believe that careful preliminary planning and research will contribute greatly to the success of your business venture. "Doing your homework" is what I call this imperative first step.

Of course, reading this book is one of the wisest things you can do to understand the intricacies of a pet-sitting business. Unlike general business books, this publication takes a hands-on approach to running a pet-sitting service. I only wish my book had been available to me when I was pondering the idea and researching the field of pet sitting!

Nonetheless, you should check out other resources. Business books have become very popular—you'll find multitudes of them at your local book store or library. These books will explain how to write a business plan (there is even a book that has a sample business plan for a pet-sitting business—see the Addenda for ordering information), ways to raise business capital and accounting for small businesses, among other things. Because of the wide availability of these types of books, I intentionally left some of these subjects out or skimmed over them in this book. That does not mean these topics don't deserve your attention while investigating the opening of your pet-sitting venture.

While visiting your local library or bookstore, spend some time perusing business magazines as well. There are many on the market today that contain informative articles on business start-ups, success stories as well as important business considerations for the small-business owner. Research should also include a search of your library's periodical files for past magazine articles on pet sitting, small businesses or home-based ventures. The trend to self-employment in recent years has created an increase in publications for entrepreneurs, many of which provide useful information.

The United States Small Business Administration (SBA) alone is a tremendous resource—I strongly recommend that you contact your local SBA office for help researching or starting your business. You'll be amazed at the wealth of information and assistance available from this government office. Your tax dollars help fund this organization, so why not take advantage of it? Write or call to get the address of a field office in your area.

United States Small Business Administration
1111 Eighteenth Street, N.W., Sixth Floor
Washington, D.C. 20036
(202) 606-4000

Through the SBA, you can receive training and guidance on everything from the basics of starting a small business and developing records and bookkeeping systems to locating sources of financing, finding customers and determining a business site. The SBA also offers informative business development publications, such as "Accounting Services for Small Service Firms," "Pricing Your Products and Services Profitably," "Planning and Goal Setting for Small Businesses," "Business Plan for Small Service Firms" and "Checklist for Going into Business." These are only a few of the many such publications available; you should obtain and digest as much basic business knowledge as you can from these offerings. Some are available free of charge; there is a nominal charge for others. All are certainly of value to the budding entrepreneur.

You also can find excellent help from retired area executives who work through the SBA in a program called SCORE (Service Corps of Retired Executives). These retirees work on a volunteer basis to help those needing assistance and counseling in the world of business. The SCORE program has been operating since 1965 and is an asset to any community because of the invaluable expertise it provides. The best part about it is that it's free! Check with your local SBA to determine if a SCORE group is located near you. You should also check with your local Chamber of Commerce, or any other business associations, to see if a similar volunteer program exists within their ranks.

A resource that is a must for anyone thinking of starting a business is the Internal Revenue Service (IRS). Call or visit your local IRS office to obtain their publication, "Taxpayers Starting a Business." This booklet explains the types of business structures available (sole proprietor versus partnership versus corporation), how to apply for an Employer Identification Number (EIN) and contains an explanation of the taxes owed by businesses. Accounting and bookkeeping systems are also discussed. This is mandatory reading for the new entrepreneur, so request this pamphlet along with any others offered by the IRS for people who are starting a business.

Your state tax department may have similar information available regarding state requirements for business owners. State taxes may include income, unemployment and sales tax. Most states do not tax personal services, such as pet sitting, but this is not true in every state.

Note: Failure to withhold, collect and pay required taxes can result in back tax assessments along with interest and penalties. Become as knowledgeable as you can about these important aspects of running a business.

If you're thinking of operating your business from your home, first check with your city or county inspections department for ordinances and restrictions governing home businesses. You should also ascertain whether a home-occupation permit is required (usually there is a small charge for this permit). At the local level, you should research city or county ordinances that specifically apply to pets and animals. Are there leash laws or litter laws in effect? As a reputable pet sitter, you want to be aware of, and in compliance with, any such ordinances.

Other recommended research and resources include:

Your Local Chamber of Commerce

Check to see if yours provides a Small Business Center. Also, request demographics of your local population, average income and so on. Inquire about mentoring programs, business seminars or workshops available to members. Obtain the phone numbers for any local retail merchants' associations and your area's Better Business Bureau; then call them to learn about the information and services they provide.

Local Technical or Community Colleges and Universities

These often have a Small Business Center or Business Extension Department that offers business courses through their continuing education department. Classes or workshops can include everything from the basics of running a small business to the psychology behind consumer choices. Sometimes local experts, such as accountants or lawyers, are available as guest speakers and will answer questions from attendees. I've taken advantage of several of these programs over the years. Some have been better than others, but all have been economical opportunities to learn. Plus, the classes were full of supportive entrepreneurial "soul mates," some of whom became clients of my pet-sitting business after meeting me in class!

Other Pet Sitters

Now that our industry is getting a little older, some veteran pet sitters provide business consultation services (for a fee) to those thinking of getting into pet sitting. These pet sitters have a wealth of experience to share and care enough about their chosen career that they want newcomers to get started on the right foot. Contact information on pet sitters who offer consultation services is available from Pet Sitters International (see page 199 for address).

Some pet sitters have even started local or regional networking groups that meet on a regular basis. If any pet-sitting services exist in your community, call them to determine if any networking meetings take place. Attending local meetings of pet sitters is an excellent way to learn about the business and to see if anyone local is interested in mentoring.

Trade Organizations

Last but certainly not least, trade organizations are a very valuable resource, and today it seems there is an organization for every profession under the sun! Of possible interest to business owners are The National Association for the Self-Employed (NASE) and The National Federation of Independent Businesses (NFIB). Female entrepreneurs may find the National Foundation of Women Business Owners to be a source of information. (Please see the Addenda for contact information.)

Until I got into business for myself, I did not realize how helpful trade organizations are or how valuable they are to an industry. Although there wasn't any such organization for pet sitters until I founded a national one for pet sitters in 1989, it (along with this book!) is something else that I wish had been available to me starting out. That's why I encourage new or "wannabe" pet sitters to immediately contact Pet Sitters International, an educational organization for professional pet sitters.

PET SITTERS INTERNATIONAL (PSI)

So what does a trade organization do that makes it so valuable to industry members? Much more than the public probably realizes. So, assuming that you are not aware of the importance of an industry association, I'd like to spend a little time enlightening you about the benefits and services available to pet-sitting industry members through Pet Sitters International.

First, understand that there is clout (power and influence) in numbers. Having an industry organization in place that is comprised of a number of industry members is impressive, not only because it lends credibility to a profession, but also because numbers get people's attention. Having a trade organization has helped us to educate the pet-owning consumers we want as clients and to make them feel comfortable in the wide availability of our services in the United States and Canada; it has also helped us to get the recognition we deserve from related businesses and industries. For example, we now have a tailor-made business liability insurance policy available to our members. Today's pet sitter doesn't have to put up with the frustration many of us endured while trying to find this important coverage for our businesses. The best part is that the insurance is offered to us at affordable group rates—because through our organization, we are a professional group!

Another stride we have made as an organized group involves the Yellow Pages of many phone directories. Years ago, there were so few of us and the industry was so new that most Yellow Page companies made us list our businesses under the heading of "Kennels." Although this was not all bad, it still did not allow us the professional distinction we were working so hard to establish. (Our educational efforts were telling pet owners to try a pet sitter, yet, when they consulted the Yellow Pages for such a service, we weren't listed where people would think to look!) So, a major letter-writing campaign was conducted to Yellow Page publishers, which resulted in new Yellow Page headings for many of our members! These examples might not seem like much but they have been great accomplishments for our new industry—important steps that have helped us to evolve into the professional, credible and viable industry that pet sitting is today. Such accomplishments translate into time- and money-saving victories for today's new pet sitter!

Support is another benefit that comes from a trade organization—support of the profession by member services, such as client referrals, quality standards and news releases pertaining to industry trends and developments. In assessing the value of such organizations as PSI, one has to look at the "big picture." Each time PSI participates in a radio, TV, newspaper or magazine interview, it provides publicity for the profession which enhances opportunities for all pet sitters. Each time we're able to negotiate a special rate for our members, it shows that our industry's business is recognized and coveted for its purchasing power. Equally as important, members can run their businesses more confidently knowing that PSI is there for them and is working to help make their pet-sitting business a success.

Education is a very valuable benefit as well. From PSI, pet sitters receive a wealth of information that deals specifically with professional pet sitting. Through a bimonthly magazine and annual convention, members have a forum within which to share experiences, tips and concerns. The camaraderie and networking that takes place among members alone is often worth the price of membership.

The pet-sitting industry has come a long way in the last few years and much of this progress is due, in large part, to the work of group efforts through such organizations as PSI. Thanks to PSI, there now is even an annual "Pet Sitter of the Year" award that is announced during "National Professional Pet Sitters Week" (the first full week of March each year).

Today's pet sitters are very fortunate to have PSI, as well as many other resources, available to them. Utilize all you can to operate your pet-sitting service efficiently and successfully.

MARKETING SURVEY

While doing your preliminary business research, you're bound to see this step mentioned in other general business books. It's a sound business step worth emphasizing here. To some extent the need for personalized, at-home pet care exists in all communities; by conducting a marketing survey, you can ascertain what interest there is in your local area. There are many ways to conduct such a survey. A good way to begin is to check the local Yellow Pages under "Kennels," "Pet Sitters," "Sitting Services" or "Dog/Cat Exercising" to determine if any other pet-sitting services already operate in your city or county. If not, you can be fairly confident that there is a need for this type of business.

You can better determine the level of interest or need by calling local veterinarians, groomers and pet store owners. Tell them about your plans, see if they know of anyone else offering such a service (some pet sitters don't advertise) and ask if they think this type of pet care would be well-received by their clients. While you have their attention, ask if they would support your efforts by telling pet owners about your services once you're up and running.

If there is another pet sitter offering services, call and ask to speak with the person. Be honest and explain you're considering entering the field. The pet sitter may provide valuable insight as to how busy the service is, whether business must be turned down and the locations in which he or she works. Ask if the pet sitter might help you get started for a consultation fee. Remember time and expertise are valuable commodities. A personal consultation with an experienced pet sitter may be worth its weight in gold.

> *Note:* Please do yourself and the industry a favor when calling other pet sitters by being honest. Many people today have "Caller ID," which tells them from what number a call is coming. I've heard from several pet sitters who were incensed that "competitors" posing as clients had called to ask questions about how their services were run. Often a seasoned pet sitter can tell just by the nature of the questions who is on the other end of the line. Old-fashioned honesty and trustworthiness are crucial in the pet-sitting business, so it's far better to start out this way and earn the respect of your colleagues by stating who you are and the purpose of your call. The worst thing that can happen is that the pet sitter will hang up on you, but the start of good rapport and a cooperative relationship could be the outcome!

> *An aside here:* Cooperative working relationships among local pet sitters may be very important in the future. This is because we're seeing a trend in the industry of one- to two-person pet-sitting services (husband and wife teams, friends, sisters and so on). Although these services could grow and expand, they are intentionally choosing to remain small to keep a more personal slant to the business and to avoid the headaches that can sometimes be associated with managing personnel. If smaller pet-sitting operations become the norm in the future, it will be increasingly important for pet sitters to work together

to fill in for each other during times of illness, emergency or vacation. Pet sitters may also realize advantages in working together at the local level by advertising cooperatively, holding fund-raisers for community animal organizations or simply meeting for lunch on an occasional basis. After all, no one understands this unique business like another pet sitter!

Returning to your market survey, you'll next want to approach actual pet owners and get their reaction to your proposed business. Find out how often they travel and what they presently do with their pets when they must leave home. Try to determine if they would be receptive to your service. Ask how much they'd be willing to pay for in-home care and what they'd expect from such a service.

You can conduct this portion of your survey by cold-calling people from the telephone book and asking if they own a pet. You could obtain permission from a shopping center to approach a random group of shoppers with your questions. A better way, though, would be to acquire a list of clients (including addresses and telephone numbers) from your veterinarian, groomer or even tax listings of dog owners. Because these samplings already own pets, it would be a more efficient way to conduct your research.

One pet sitter I know purchased a mailing list of subscribers in her city from a pet magazine. She then sent out an initial customer query form to these prospective customers, informing them of her new business venture and inquiring about their interest in using her service. She included a preprinted postcard that allowed them to quickly answer her questions and register their pet(s) with her company for future sittings. Not only did she receive lots of encouraging comments, but she got several definite customers before she even opened for business.

While doing your market research, don't forget to canvass your friends as well. You can usually count on friends to be honest because they want you to be happy and successful. They'll tell you if they think your idea is a good one, if the concept will go over in your area and if they think you're cut out for this type of work. Invite their opinions and then listen objectively.

Instead of "shopping the competition" by calling other pet sitters and posing as a client, try shopping your friends! By this I mean offer your pet-sitting services free of charge to a few pet-owning friends. Let them see firsthand the quality of services you plan to provide and then give them the chance to critique you. These "trial runs" will be a wise investment of your time, plus you'll have some references to use when the general public starts calling.

Once you've conducted your market survey, analyzed the results, done some "gratis" pet sitting and received honest feedback from friends or family members, you can more knowledgeably and confidently determine if a pet-sitting business is needed in your community—and if it's the right business for you. Make good notes regarding the statistics you gather during this survey. They may be useful in writing a business plan—especially if you'll be borrowing any operating capital to get your business started.

NAMING YOUR BUSINESS

Selecting a name for your pet-sitting service is an important first step. Put your thinking cap on—this task is not as easy as you might think. Keep in mind that the name of your business creates a crucial first impression. Make sure the name you choose conveys a positive image with which you'll be proud to be associated.

Name selection has become a more difficult task in recent years. When I opened my pet-sitting service in 1983, there were so few services in operation that I had a wide choice of cute, catchy names available to me. Today, with the increasing number of new pet-sitting businesses, some names are trademarked and totally off limits ōr use by others. Therefore, it's a good idea to come up with several names for your business: In the event that your first choice is not available, you'll be ready with other options.

Once you've narrowed down your name selections to two or three favorites, you'll need to check with your local Register of Deeds to see if your first choice of name is in use by a business in your community. If the name is locally available to you, your next inquiry should be to the Secretary of State's office to determine if anyone in your state has registered a business under your preferred name. If not, you'll probably have free and clear right to do business under that name in your state.

At this point, the only hitch with being able to use the name would be if it was already trademarked with the United States Patent and Trademark Office (PTO) in Washington, D.C. You can determine if there's a federal trademark on the name by visiting the PTO and checking registrations, or by hiring a patent and trademark attorney to do this verification for you. In some cities, there are search services available that will check the name for a fee. Some libraries can do a computerized patent search for you. It's a specialized service, and a fee may be involved.

Although there is some expense involved in making sure you have the right to use a business name, this can be a wise initial investment. I know of one pet sitter in Florida who had been doing business under a certain name for more than a year. She had established an excellent reputation and developed a devoted clientele. Out of the blue one day a letter arrived from an attorney in the midwest informing her to cease and desist use of her business's name immediately because it was federally trademarked (or owned) by his client. To make a long story short, the Florida pet sitter had to hire an attorney in the matter only to find that indeed, she did not have the right to do business under her current name. The innocent mistake ended up being a very costly one; it was expensive to change all of her forms, stationery and business literature. Having to acclimate her clients to a new name was awkward as well. She told me it would have been much cheaper to go through all the proper name-checking channels at the outset—not to mention the headaches she would have been spared.

Once you've decided on a name and found it available, consider how you can best protect the name for your business. Discuss how to do this with an attorney because it's a very serious subject. With the anticipated growth of the pet-sitting industry, you don't want any surprises in your mailbox in the years to come. And, you'll want the legal backing to be able to protect your good name and reputation should another pet sitter try to infringe upon it.

One way to begin protection of your name is to go to your local Register of Deeds office and register the name as a business in your community. There will be a nominal charge for the registration.

BUSINESS LOGO

Many business owners like to develop an identifiable signature or trademark for their company. A logo can be simply a set of letters, or it can include graphics. One of the best-known logos is probably the "golden arches" made famous by the McDonald's hamburger chain. If you want to establish a logo for your pet-sitting service, consider doing so at the outset. There are two reasons for developing your logo early. If you plan to federally trademark your name, it may be wise to trademark the logo along with it. Secondly, it's cost-effective to have the logo printed on your company materials at the outset rather than add it piecemeal later.

If you're creative and skilled in the use of a computer, there are many software programs that offer clip art you can use to design your own logo. Office-supply stores usually sell pads or packages of clip art for use in the public domain. Consider hiring a graphic artist or aspiring art student in your area to develop a logo for your business. Use the logo on all of your company literature and advertising to create a distinct professional image for your business.

> *Note:* Please be aware of copyright and trademark law when designing a logo. In other words, don't think you can use the McDonald's golden arches for your company's logo—nor can you copy something from a book or magazine just because you think it's cute.

BUSINESS LICENSE

Your next step will be to check with your city and county offices to determine if a license to do business is required. Most communities issue these licenses for a small fee and a little paperwork; some require that the license be visibly displayed in your place of business. Remember that if you'll be operating a home-based pet-sitting service, a home occupation permit may be required before a city/county business license will be issued to you.

As an upstanding citizen running a legitimate business, you'll need to obtain the proper business license(s) for your pet-sitting service. If you're unsure where to find out what is necessary in the way of licenses, check your local telephone directory under "Government" or "City/County" headings for the appropriate offices.

Please understand that a city/county business license is simply a tax-generating permit authorizing you to do business in your area. It in no way indicates your knowledge or abilities as a professional pet sitter. However, through the years there has been a trend by some pet sitters to list this business license as a credential on their business cards and company literature. This has become a pet peeve of mine—I think it is misleading to the public. Usually when we see the term "licensed" we tend to think of a state exam or course of study being required prior to the obtainment of the license. Because, as of this writing, there is no regulatory licensing required of professional pet sitters, use of the term is misrepresentative. There is now a voluntary accreditation program available to pet sitters through PSI that does involve a self-paced home study program with a proctored test that must be passed for certification. This is a much more meaningful business credential with which to honestly impress the general public.

OFFICE LOCATION

You will need to determine the location for your pet-sitting service. The service, especially in the beginning, can easily be run from your home (if, as discussed earlier, home-based businesses are permitted in your residential area). A spare bedroom, basement area or even a large closet should be adequate. You need only a small space to set up your operation. In the past, there have been tax advantages to operating a business from home. Because tax laws change frequently, get advice from a tax professional concerning advantages of operating a business from your home.

If the idea of basing your business in your home appeals to you, give careful thought as to whether you can work well in your home. Can you discipline yourself to work, or will there be too many distractions and temptations to keep you from giving your business the time and effort required? Also, a large part of a pet-sitting service is conducted over the telephone, and calls can come at all hours. To keep work from disrupting your home life, you will have to be able to separate these two areas and think of the office as a workplace with its own hours.

Will you be running your pet-sitting service alone, or will you have a partner who will share the work load? If you have a partner, this may be a factor in determining where your office is located. A partner or office assistant may not feel comfortable or be able to work efficiently from your home. Will there be other pet-sitting staff members who will be traipsing in and out of your home? This could be bothersome to other family members and could result in complaints from neighbors as well. Are there small children who may decide to throw a tantrum while you're trying to sell your services to an inquirer? Give careful thought to your office location at the outset. Be sure of your location before having your business address and phone number printed; making changes on printed literature can be costly.

If you can work out the details to base your business in your home, it can be convenient and usually much cheaper to operate. In fact, the establishment of home-based businesses of all types is a fast-growing phenomenon as more and more people discover the advantages of working at home. Almost 30 million Americans work part- or full-time at home, according to Link Resources Corporation, a New York–based group that studies the trend.

If you prefer to locate your business outside your home, remember that you do not need the plushest surroundings for an office space. All you need at the beginning is an area large enough to accommodate a desk (or card table) for your phone and a bookcase or shelf (or another card table) for your supplies, files and resource materials. It is rare for a customer to visit your office, so appearances are not critical. Look for the most reasonable rent in a convenient and safe area of town where you'll look forward to working. A final word of advice is to remember that rents and lease terms are not carved in stone. Don't be afraid to negotiate—you might find a landlord is willing to be flexible to secure a good tenant.

LEGAL STRUCTURE

Another important consideration in starting your pet-sitting service is how to legally structure your business. The choices available for business organizations include sole proprietorship, general partnership or limited partnership, corporations (C corporations and S corporations) and limited liability companies (LLCs). Tax consequences and liabilities vary with each of these legal structures. Seek advice from professionals (attorney, accountant, tax consultant) before deciding which structure is the best for you and your business.

> *Note:* It is entirely possible to determine your business's legal structure and incorporate your business (if that is your choice) by yourself, just as you can do the research and leg work to register your business's name and obtain business licenses. This way you save attorney fees and lower your start-up costs. However, I strongly recommend that you at least consult with an attorney regarding these business matters and decisions. Usually there's little or no charge for a consultation, and the discussion will help you make informed decisions about your business. A reliable attorney and accountant can be instrumental in your business's well-being. You are wise to cultivate good relationships with both at the very outset of your new venture. In other words, let key people do what they do best to help you do your best.

FINDING AN ACCOUNTANT

Here again, unless you're an experienced bookkeeper, it is advisable to find an accountant to assist you with the necessary record keeping for your pet-sitting service. Look for one who specializes in accounting for small businesses, because that's what you'll be for the first few years. An accountant will help you set up your books, do your payroll and apply for any necessary identification numbers. An accountant can also save you some running around by supplying the forms you'll need, such as state and federal payroll tax forms. Although accounting procedures may at first seem overwhelming to a new business owner, a good accountant will soon have you trained and knowledgeable about the financial side of your business.

Shop around when searching for an accountant. Ask other business owners for recommendations and then interview a few accountants before making a decision. Accounting fees and expertise vary, so don't be shy in requesting fees, credentials and references from candidates. Make sure the individual is someone you feel you can trust and with whom you can get along. If you find yourself unhappy with an accountant, remember that you are not locked into his or her services, and you can take your business elsewhere.

SELECTING A BANK

A business checking account is necessary for your pet-sitting service. Here again, it pays to shop around before making a decision. Different banks offer various features and hours of operation. You should take into account the convenience of the bank's location. Once your pet-sitting services become popular, you'll have little time to waste when making bank deposits. Some banks advertise specifically to attract small business owners. Find out what, if any, services they provide that may directly benefit you.

Explore the possibility of obtaining a credit card exclusively for your business's use. In today's business world, a credit card can come in handy when making large purchases for your business, traveling to workshops and conventions or simply entertaining clients or staff members. Also, by paying your account on time, the credit card helps you establish a credit history for your business.

Will the bank extend you a line of credit or overdraft protection? This can be important to sustain you during any lull in business or in allowing you to make investments in your business, such as advertising campaigns or computer equipment.

Also find out whether the bank will issue a merchant card to you. This allows you to accept Visa and MasterCard from clients as payment for services. Although traditionally most pet sitters have only accepted cash or personal checks as methods of payment, there is an increasing trend in the industry, especially from larger pet-sitting companies, to accept charge cards for payment. There are advantages and disadvantages to accepting "plastic," so obtain details from your banker so you can carefully consider this option for your business.

Allot the proper amount of time to explore banking services for your business, even down to the details of what type of checks and deposit slips are available. (Many pet sitters like to order animal or pet-theme checks to use in their business.) It's important to spend this time during your planning stages, because after your business is up and running, your time truly does become more limited.

INSURANCE

It is smart and advisable to obtain liability insurance to cover you and any other pet sitters working in your business. Hopefully, you'll never need to use this insurance, but having the coverage will give you and your customers peace of mind. And, very importantly, it is often a selling point to interested but hesitant customers.

Since the first edition of this book, many people have written to me indicating that they have had a difficult time finding commercial liability insurance for their pet-sitting businesses. I can empathize with them because I, too, had a difficult time obtaining such insurance when I first opened my service.

The reason it has been difficult to find coverage is that pet sitting has been a relatively new profession with unique insurance needs. A pet-sitting business is unlike a kennel operation that insures its premises for accidents and damages. Instead, a pet sitter needs protection that insures the premises of each client where he or she is conducting business. Our need is similar to that of a janitorial or cleaning service that visits various locations for the performance of duties. However, our liability coverage also needs to extend to the animals entrusted to our care.

Many insurance companies have never heard of the pet-sitting industry and, therefore, won't have a policy already available to meet your specific needs. Although this doesn't mean an insurance policy cannot be created that is tailored to your business, you need to be prepared to explain the nature of the pet-sitting business and to ask if a policy can be designed specifically for you. If you have an insurance agent with whom you've done business in the past, contact him or her first for help in this area. If they've written automobile or homeowner's insurance for you, they know a little about you. To keep your business, they may be more willing to seek out the proper coverage that meets the needs of your pet-sitting business.

Still, it's going to be hard to beat the Pet Sitters Liability Protection Policy that was written for pet sitters and is offered, at group rates, through PSI. I strongly advise new pet sitters to take advantage of this plan. It is a real coup for our industry that we now have it available. It saves you time in locating good coverage, and it saves you money by being a group plan. Another insurance concern you should look into regards your automobile coverage. Because you'll most likely be doing a lot more driving as a professional pet sitter, find out if your car insurance is adequate. Many pet sitters purchase an insurance rider that provides additional coverage in the event of an automobile accident when pet sitting. This type of coverage is triggered only if the pet sitter's personal automobile insurance coverage is not adequate for damages incurred. This coverage can be very important if you will have staff pet sitters working for your company. Find out if your company's rider will extend to their vehicles, just in case. We do live in a lawsuit mad society!

If you'll be hiring employees to help you with pet-sitting visits, you'll also need to investigate Worker's Compensation insurance in your state. Most states require some form of this insurance, and your personal insurance agent or state Department of Labor can tell you what applies to your business. This type of insurance covers the employees of a business should they be injured while working.

> *Note:* States classify workers by assigning a code to them, which is used to assign Workman's Compensation rates to various occupations. As of this writing, there is not a uniform classification applied to pet sitters. Therefore, some states, for lack of understanding or appropriate classifications, consider pet sitters similar to janitors while others classify us as kennel assistants! Check into how your state classifies pet sitters—it could make a big impact on what you are charged for this coverage.

As your business grows, you should review your life insurance coverage. Make sure it would be sufficient to keep your business going in the event of your death and that it would cover any debts owed by your business for which your estate may be accountable. Life insurance may not have been important to you before, but it is something you should consider as a business owner.

While surveying your insurance needs, do some cost comparisons—coverages and rates can vary among insurance companies. Besides, each phone call you make will help to educate more insurance agents about our growing industry. And who knows? The agent may be a local pet owner who would be interested in using your service!

DISHONESTY BOND

Many people are familiar with the term "bonded," yet few understand what it really means. Because it is just as important to the professional pet sitter as having good liability insurance, I want to take a few minutes to discuss bonding in laymen's terms.

Simply defined, a *bond* is a form of insurance that protects the business owner (and, in pet sitting, the customer) in the event of theft. However, unlike insurance, if a bond company makes payment, it usually expects restitution of the amount paid either from the business owner or the convicted party. From where the restitution is expected is very important to you, as a business owner, in purchasing a bond. If you plan to utilize staff pet sitters in your business, you'll sleep much better knowing that if one of your pet sitters is convicted of theft, your bond will reimburse your client (up to the amount payable by your bond). Your bonding company will then go after the convicted pet sitter to recoup the money it paid for his or her theft. Make sure this is the type of bond you purchase—you don't want the company to expect you to reimburse it for a loss due to someone else's actions.

This type of bond, recommended for pet sitters, is presently available from a well-known surety company that works with members of PSI. This company has also provided a rider to PSI members who operate their business as sole proprietors. Although many bonding companies will not extend a bond to the owner of a business, this particular one has made an exception because so many pet-sitting firms are owner-operated.

How much of a bond should you consider purchasing for your pet-sitting business? This is a personal business decision. If you'll be working alone and doing all the pet-sitting visits yourself, you may want to purchase only a small bond in the amount of $5,000 or $10,000. (This assumes you know that you are honest and trustworthy, so you're only purchasing a minimum bond as a good faith effort for your business.) If you plan to use a staff of pet sitters or if you pet sit in very affluent areas, a higher bond might be advisable.

A concern of new pet sitters that I often hear is, "What's to stop someone from setting me up and accusing me of stealing from their home just to collect some money?" This is a legitimate concern and one that worried me, too, at the outset. What you need to understand though is that it's not that easy to do. For a dishonesty bond to pay out, a person has to be tried and convicted of the crime—it takes more than just an accusation. It is not a pleasant, fast or easy way to make some money. Still, as the owner of a service business that visits strangers' homes, you'll be smart to go this extra step and take out a dishonesty bond. The cost is nominal when you consider the peace of mind it provides for you and your customer. And, being bonded and insured speaks well for the professionalism and integrity of your business and for our industry as a whole.

> *Note:* As a business owner who is responsible for the pet sitters you send into customer homes, you'll be wise to do thorough background checks to make sure the people you hire are honest, reliable and trustworthy. Checking references is discussed in more detail in Chapter 4, "Personnel."

BASIC OFFICE SUPPLIES AND FURNISHINGS

There are a few basic furnishings and supplies you'll need for your business office before officially opening your pet-sitting service. Try to keep your office needs to a minimum to reduce your overhead costs. You can pass on these savings to your customers in lower pet-sitting rates. (Lower rates may result in a higher volume of customers, which will contribute to the success of your business.) Recommended office basics include:

- Table or desk

- Chair(s)

- Bookcase (shelf or space for supplies)

- Telephone (See the "Business Telephone" section at the end of this chapter.)

- Telephone answering machine or answering service

- City map (one for the office and one for your car—a city map is helpful for determining service routes, as well as for getting you to your clients' homes)

- Calculator (a basic model that adds, subtracts, multiplies and divides should suffice—one with paper tape comes in handy when adding deposits)

- Name and address rubber stamp (handy for endorsing checks and pre-addressing envelopes for customers to use when paying— don't forget the necessary ink pad)

- Typewriter or computer with a word-processing program.

Note: A typewriter or computer is nice but is not absolutely necessary to have. If you don't have access to one, or don't type, you can hire a typist (look in the classified ads of your newspaper or in the Yellow Pages). You can have any necessary forms typeset at a printing company or purchase them camera-ready from a pet-sitting supply company.

- Filing cabinet (a must for storing such paperwork as service con-tracts, forms and advertising that is associated with your business— if you'll be storing client house keys in it, get one with a lock)

- Schedule book and calendar (absolutely necessary to keep up with customer appointments, sitting assignments and so on—*write it down,* or you'll find yourself needing to pick up two sets of house keys at the same time on opposite ends of town . . . which is a little hard to do)

- Reference books and educational videos on various pets and their care (Some of these may be available from your local library. Familiarize yourself with different types of animals, reptiles and various breeds. When a customer calls and asks what you charge for caring for a Maltese, you'll know it's a dog and not a falcon!)

- First-aid supplies for humans (Band-Aids for paper cuts!) or pet emergencies

You will need the following paper supplies:

- Index cards and storage box

- Stationery (professionally printed with your business name, address, phone number and any logo or slogan you want to associate with your business)

- Envelopes matching your stationery. You may want to pick a color scheme and use it everywhere your name is seen. The repetition will help make your business recognizable to your public.

- Envelopes (white business envelopes you can address with your rubber stamp to leave for your customers to remit payment)

- Business cards. Get these professionally printed because you will use them a lot to advertise your business. You want them to look nice and to convey a good first impression to potential clients. They are relatively inexpensive.

- A flyer or brochure that gives basic information about what your service provides. This is a valuable advertising tool you'll use often. This item is discussed in more detail in Chapter 5, "Advertising."

- Notepads (plain or matching your other stationery). You will use these primarily for leaving your clients notes and, of course, for phone messages.

- Accounting ledger. This is a columnar book that your accountant will most likely supply and explain to you unless you are using a computer software program for your bookkeeping.

- Five-columnar accounting pad. This ledger is available in most office supply stores. These sheets contain lined pages you can use to chart sitter schedules. Or, you may prefer to purchase a camera-ready Sitter Schedule Sheet (which I used in my business and now sell through my pet-sitting supply company—see the Addenda for ordering information) or to utilize a software program for this task.

- Business forms. You will need at least a well-thought out service contract for your business, and there are other forms that will be helpful as well. These are discussed further in Chapter 8, "Useful Business Forms."

Other standard office supplies you'll need include:

- Pens and pencils
- Scissors
- Ruler
- Tape
- Postage stamps
- Labels for folders and house keys

- Paper clips
- Stapler
- File folders
- Staple remover
- Hanging file folders
- Correction fluid

Your office supplies need not be brand new. If you have an extra pair of scissors around the house, loan them to your business. For anything you purchase for your business, make sure you keep the receipt. Any legitimate office and business expenses will need to be accounted for at tax time. Keep your business supplies as pet-related as possible. Your logo, stationery and business cards, for example, can easily be designed to reflect the nature of your business. As previously mentioned, try to order checks that have pets, animals or wildlife pictured on them. Also, purchase stamps that feature pets or wildlife. I have used such checks and stamps for years and have found that people really do notice the coordinated details of my business. Just be sure not to sacrifice professionalism for what I call "cutesiness."

Although your clients will furnish most of the things you'll need to properly care for their pet(s), there are some recommended supplies that will be helpful while in the course of actually pet sitting. These are detailed in Chapter 4, in the "Sitter Orientation" and "Survival Items" sections.

BUSINESS TELEPHONE

In conclusion, a word about your business telephone: Some pet sitters operating from home have made the mistake of using their personal telephone number as their business line. This is not such a good idea for several reasons. First, your telephone company will not appreciate your disregard for any policy they may have regarding business lines. There could even be a tariff violation or penalty if it learns of your home-based business. Second, although a business line does normally cost more than a residential line, you also usually get a free Yellow Page listing for your business. This exposure can really help to increase the calls you'll receive for service. After all, if you've named your business "XYZ Pet Sitters" but your phone number is only listed under your name, Mary Doe, how is the public going to find you? Your credibility as a reputable business could be damaged by a potential client's inability to find your number in the phone book or through information. Third, as your business grows, your phone will be ringing more and more. Calls will come in at all hours. Because you'll have no way of knowing whether the call is of a personal or business nature, you'll find yourself answering the phone and possibly beginning to feel that you have no privacy. Prevent this problem by ordering a legitimate business line from the outset of your pet-sitting venture. That way, you can distinguish callers and answer your business line only during your regularly scheduled office hours. Finally, your business phone bill will be an expense of doing business and, as such, can be claimed on your income tax return. By having a separate billing for your business line, your record and receipt keeping will also be a much easier task.

Note: Many customers will memorize your business phone number. Get a number that you plan to keep for years to come and one that's easy to remember as well. Have the entire phone number or the last four digits spell out "PETS" or "DOGS" or "CATS" or "LOVE"— something identifiable with your service!

You may be wondering if you'll need either a telephone answering machine or personal answering service for your business. Yes, you will need one of these methods for taking messages. The merits of each will be discussed further in the following chapter.

CHAPTER 3

OFFICE PROCEDURES

CUSTOMER CARD SYSTEM

Whether you work alone or you have twelve sitters working with you, you'll need an organized system in order to run your office efficiently. The system developed and used successfully in my office may seem simple and elementary, but it works. You may want to expand or improve upon it, but it will provide a means of getting started. First, the index cards and storage box (mentioned in Chapter 2, in the "Basic Office Supplies and Furnishings" section) make up your customer card box. When receiving calls for pet-sitting services, you'll need to make a customer card for each client. The sample shown here indicates some of the pertinent information you should gather when the reservation is made. Write this data in pencil to allow for any necessary changes. You'll find that last names, addresses, phone numbers and even pets do change. After you've checked the schedules and assigned a sitter to the job, notify the customer who his or her sitter will be and pencil in the sitter's name in the right-hand corner of the card. Place the card in a stack of "jobs to notify sitters about" by the telephone.

SITTER SCHEDULE SHEETS

After promptly contacting the appropriate sitter for each job, turn to your sitter schedule sheets. A schedule is made on each sitter using the

```
Customer Name                           Sitter's Name
Address
City, State Zip Code


Home phone number:
Work phone number:


Type of pet(s):                    Price:
Visits requested per day:
Dates of services:
How did you hear about our service?
```

five-columnar accounting pad mentioned in the section "Basic Office Supplies and Furnishings." The sample that follows shows how I suggest you label your assignment sheets. Only after you've given the sitter information about the upcoming assignment do you fill in the customer's name and dates of the assignment on the sheet. This is your way of making sure you've assigned it. Then, place the customer card in a designated space for pending jobs, sorted by the month and week in which they occur.

Having an assignment sheet for each sitter permits you to see at a glance how many jobs he or she has and guards against overbooking a person. You'll also need to fill in any vacation time or other dates of unavailability on each sheet to help you in assigning jobs. If a sitter has requested assignments for only cats or specializes in birds or the care of exotics, you can denote this information at the top of each sitter's schedule sheet. The information will help you, or your office manager, in making the best match according to a client's pet-care needs. The next step is to check customer cards daily in the ongoing/pending stacks to see which jobs have ended; then place these cards vertically and alphabetically in your customer card box. This tells you the jobs are finished but not yet paid for.

As payments arrive in the office, record the date and amount of payment; then, turn the card horizontally in the customer card box. Next, write the date and amount paid by the customer on the sitter's schedule sheet. After endorsing the checks, make your bank deposit. When it's time to write payroll or commission checks, you'll use the "payment

Sitter Schedule Sheet

Sitter's Name,
Address, and Phone Number
Areas of Service Route

Customer Name	Dates of Service	Job Completed	Payment Received	Sitter Paid	New★ Customer?
K. Smith	7/1/86 7/7/86	✔	7/10/86 54.00	✔ 8/1/86	★

Vacation of Sitter 8/8/86   8/15/86
12/10/86   12/12/86

UNPAID ACCOUNTS

PAID ACCOUNTS

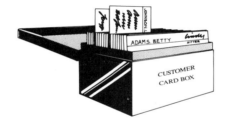

received" column on the sitter schedule sheets. Always write the date the customer's check was received in this column. By referring to this column each month, you can easily see for which jobs the sitter is due payment. Write the date the sitter was compensated in the "sitter paid" column. And this, in a nutshell, is the system I used in my pet-sitting service. Simple enough? The following flow chart illustrates my system to clarify the steps even further.

Note: If you're treating your pet sitters as independent contractors, your business and accounting procedures will need to be structured differently to meet the guidelines set forth by the Internal Revenue Service. A knowledgeable accountant can explain the advantages and disadvantages of using independent contractors for assignments and how to do your record keeping if this is the staffing method you choose.

Office Procedures Flow Chart

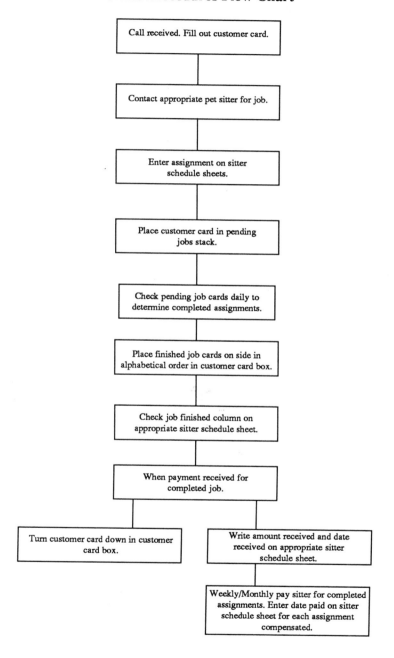

HANDLING DELINQUENT ACCOUNTS

By keeping the customer cards turned vertically on their side until payment is received, it's easy to do a weekly check to see if any accounts are becoming delinquent. If more than an acceptable amount of time for payment has passed, you may want to call the customer or mail out a friendly past due letter. Samples of such letters follow.

Delinquent Account Letter #1

Dear Client:

A review of our records indicates a delinquent balance on your account of $_____. This amount is due for our pet-sitting services provided by Molly Smith, from July 7 through July 14, 1996. We hope this has simply been an oversight on your part. We enjoyed caring for your pets and would like to continue sitting for you in the future. Therefore, we thank you in advance for remitting payment to us within the next five (5) days.

Very truly yours,

XYZ Pet Sitters, Inc.

Delinquent Account Letter #2

Dear (Client's Name):

A review of our records shows that you owe a balance of $_____ for XYZ Pet Sitters, Inc., services rendered _____ through _____. We believe there are two sides to every story, so if you'll be so kind as to listen to our side, we'll listen to your side.

Our Side	Your Side
We provided XYZ Pet Sitter services which you requested in a reliable, trustworthy and caring manner. Our service contract plainly states that payment is due within 3 days after a customer returns from a trip. We regret that in an effort to reduce our	

overhead costs and keep our service affordable, we are not able
to extend credit.

If you were pleased with our
services, we shall appreciate
your prompt remittance of fees
owed. If you were not pleased,
we shall appreciate hearing your
side in the right-hand column of
this page.

We appreciate your cooperation and hope that you've just for-
gotten about your balance owed.
We look forward to your continued business.

Very truly yours,
XYZ Pet Sitters, Inc.

My experience has shown, though, that delinquent accounts are not
much of a problem; 99.9 percent of my customers promptly paid their
bills after using our services. I like to think that our excellent collection
record is a direct reflection on the quality of our service. Perhaps clients
are so pleased that they immediately paid their bills to stay on our good
side. I've also come to believe over the years that people who love their
pets enough to hire a pet sitter are not the kind of people who write bad
checks or ignore their financial obligations. The occasional straggler I
had was usually a client who traveled so frequently that he or she had
simply not been home long enough to sit down and pay all the bills. The
stragglers, though, almost always came through and usually included a
nice tip as an apology for their lateness. Sometimes it pays to be flexible
with your payment terms for unusual situations.

To protect myself against late or nonpaying customers, I included a
clause in our service contract that said when payment was due and noted
that a monthly interest rate would be charged on accounts unpaid in excess
of thirty days. I also stated that a penalty would be charged on any checks
returned from the bank. Perhaps I was lucky, but I had very few checks
returned from the bank for insufficient funds. After I notified the clients,
they immediately made the checks good. There are some pet sitters who

require full payment in advance, especially from new clients. Although this idea has merit and may be more of a necessity in large metropolitan areas, I never instituted the practice in my business. It's my belief that pet owners should be able to use the service, make sure they are pleased and then pay their bill within a timely manner. I always tried to put myself in the customer's shoes, and there was something disconcerting to me about being required to pay in advance for something with which I might not be happy. New clients in particular may feel uneasy about up-front payment. However, once they try your service and are pleased, don't be surprised to find that they leave advance payment for you on the kitchen counter for subsequent home visits.

The only situations in which I did require any advance payment were lengthy assignments that exceeded a certain dollar amount. When this was the case, I insisted that half of the bill be paid. My reasoning here is that the longer the assignment, the greater the chance for extra expense: more food or supplies may be needed; the pet may become ill and require veterinary care; or something could go wrong at the home, requiring the services of a plumber or electrician. Should any of these things occur, I would have money from the client with which to cover these costs without dipping into the company's bank account. Any additional money owed by the client was then paid upon the client's return. It's not unreasonable to require a deposit on lengthy assignments; however it is your business, so you'll need to set your own payment policy and be sure it is one with which you can live.

SMALL CLAIMS COURT

Should you have any problem or dispute in collecting payment from a client, remember that you do have the recourse of small claims court. (In small claims court, a magistrate hears cases in which the amount involved doesn't exceed a certain figure, such as $1,500.00. The specific amount varies state by state.) Sometimes just threatening to take the client to court is enough to secure payment. But, if necessary, don't hesitate to use the recourse of small claims court. Taking someone who owes you money to court is a simple, straightforward process, and relatively inexpensive. The only inconvenience may be the time required to sit in court until your case can be presented. So, if you believe in the job that you did for the client and have exhausted other civil means of collecting the payment rightfully due you, by all means, take the client to court.

Being a person of principle, I did utilize small claims court a couple of times during the ten years I operated my pet-sitting business. The first time involved a client who had contracted with us for a lengthy sitting assignment during the Christmas and New Year's holiday period. The job involved caring for a large breed dog who was to be visited daily with morning and evening visits. As fate would have it, our weather turned bad for a few days during this period and we experienced some ice and snow which made travel hazardous. Still, my pet sitter assigned to the job risked the hazardous travel to fulfill every visit as contracted. When the client returned home, he called our office ranting and raving that his dog had destroyed his backdoor by chewing and scratching. He insisted that this damage was the fault of our service. Not only did he refuse to pay his bill of more than $200.00, he also insisted that we replace his backdoor to the tune of $500.00. I discussed the situation with the pet sitter, and she confirmed that she had noticed some scratches on the back door but thought they had been there. She also said the dog was very energetic so such mischievousness was not out of the ordinary for a large breed confined to inside quarters. Because damages due to pets is a risk that all pet owners face when acquiring a pet and because my service did not provide, or contract to provide, 24-hour-a-day care where the pet would be watched every minute, I thought the client was unfair in his assessment of liability and refusal to pay his bill. So, I filed a claim for the money he owed us in small claims court. He countered with a claim asking for money to buy a new back door, and to court we went. Yes, I was nervous and had no idea what to expect, yet I firmly believed we were being unjustly accused of something that was not our fault. After all, a female dog in heat could have crossed the back yard and caused our client's dog to try to tear the back door down. Or someone could have tried to enter the back door (such as an intruder) which caused the dog to go berserk. And because the client was later in returning than anticipated, any damages he was trying to find us liable for could have occurred between the time we made our last visit and his arrival home. There were just too many variables. Fortunately, after hearing both sides, the magistrate ruled in our favor, telling the client to pay his bill and our court costs associated with filing the claim.

When an award is made in small claims court, a lien is filed against the person found at fault. When this judgment is paid, the lien is removed from the person's record showing that the debt has been satisfied. In my case, the client paid the pet-sitting bill but failed to pay the court costs, so the lien stayed on his record. Five years later, the client wanted to sell his house. A buyer was found but before the transaction occurred, court records were checked to make sure no liens were held against the home. Guess what showed up? A debt of $29.00 that was still owed to my pet-sitting service! The client could not sell his house until this was paid and the lien was removed.

MORE ACCOUNT COLLECTION TIPS

At a pet-sitting convention I recently attended, delinquent accounts were discussed with the following collection methods suggested by other pet sitters:

- Don't return the client's house key until you have been paid!
- If you have to send a second delinquent account letter, mail it certified to the customer. The client will then have to sign for the letter, which makes it seem to be of greater importance!
- Show up on the client's doorstep and explain that because you were in the neighborhood, you decided to drop by and pick up the payment due you.
- Ask your 300-pound cousin, Vinny, to stop by and collect the payment!

POLICIES AND PROCEDURES

Every business has established policies, and your pet-sitting service should not be an exception. As a business owner, there are going to be decisions you will have to make regarding the way your business operates. Just as you'll need to determine what your payment policy is (such as within five days after client returns, thirty days from contract's starting or ending date and so on), there are many other issues you will have to determine. Some of these you can decide in advance, while others may surface as time goes by. My recommendation is that you actually put your company policies and operating procedures in writing. When a client asks why you don't make pet-sitting visits at midnight, you can honestly explain that it's company policy to finish all pet care rounds prior to 8:30 P.M. (or whatever time you elect) due to concerns about sitter safety. A Policy and Procedures Manual will also be informative if you hire an office manager or pet sitters to assist you. Having written policies and procedures to refer to will help employees to learn about your company and what is expected of them.

Things you should consider when setting policies and efficient operating procedures include the following:

- Payment policy. Will you require deposits? How long will clients have to pay their bill? Will you charge interest on late accounts or fees for returned checks? Will you accept charge cards?

- Pet-sitting visit hours. Will you make pet-care visits at any time requested by the customer, or will you make them within certain time parameters?

- Office hours. When can clients expect to reach someone at your business phone or expect to have their call returned?

- Pet immunizations. What is your policy regarding immunizations you'll require of pets under your care?

- House key maintenance and returns. How will you maintain security of house keys in your possession? Will you charge extra to personally pick up or return a house key?

- Initial client interviews. Will you charge clients for initial introductory interviews? How long will you typically spend, or expect your staff to spend, while conducting an initial interview?

- Job sharing. Will only one sitter be assigned to each client or will one sitter do morning rounds while another sitter makes the evening round? Will you accept assignments where a neighbor or family member is asked to provide some of the pet care during the owner's absence?

- Leash walking. Will you require that all dogs you are asked to walk be kept on a leash?

- Pet identification. Will your policy be that all dogs and cats under your care wear some form of identification?

- Last minute reservations. Will you accept them if it means you won't have the opportunity to do an in-home consultation with the client and pet? Will you charge extra for last minute reservations?

- Holiday surcharges. Will you charge extra for visits made on major holidays?

This is by no means a complete list of policies and procedures to be considered in a pet-sitting business; however, it is an excellent starting point that hopefully will get you headed in the right direction. As stated earlier, there isn't any one way to run a pet-sitting service, although some ways are better than others! I suggest that as you read this book, you make notes along the way of circumstances where a written policy will be smart to have in place. And, don't forget—policies can always be changed! What works in the beginning for you may need some revision as you, and your service, learn and grow.

TELEPHONE TECHNIQUES

The telephone plays a vital role in your business; the majority of your business is handled over the telephone. Customers call to get information about your service and to book your services. A phone conversation may be the first impression a client gets of your business, so telephone etiquette is extremely important. Your local telephone company may provide you with business phone tips, so ask if it also provides business etiquette advice. Here are some pointers I can share with you:

- Answer your phone quickly—after two rings if possible.
- Identify your company name and who's speaking (XYZ Pet Sitting Service, Jane Smith speaking).
- Speak in a courteous, friendly, confident tone.
- Smile as you speak! You may feel silly at first, but it really reflects in your tone of voice.
- Provide as much information as possible about your service. Remember that the inquirer called you and wants to understand your services.
- Patiently try to answer all of the client's questions. It's only natural for a potential new client to have some reservations about using your service and allowing a stranger into the home.
- When using an answering machine, personalize your message and say when customer calls will be returned.
- Return customer calls promptly. This goes for you and your sitters. The sooner, the better!
- Use the phone to obtain as much initial information as possible about an assignment. Fill out your customer card completely during the phone conversation.

If you're going to run your pet-sitting service from your home, I have two pieces of telephone advice. Please have your voice mail or answering machine identify the name of your pet-sitting service when it answers calls and please, please, please, do not allow children to answer your business calls. Nothing takes the "professional" out of pet sitter faster than to hear a residence recording or to have a young child babble into the phone.

Telephone skills are so important in a service business, so practice and sharpen yours to ensure the success of your pet-sitting venture.

Sample Narrative

(For giving out information over the telephone about your services)

Caller: I saw your ad in the Yellow Pages and wondered if you could tell me a little about how your service works.

Pet sitter: What we/I do is provide personalized at-home pet care. We/I actually come to your home so you are able to leave your pet in familiar surroundings. We/I try to follow your pet care routine as closely as possible. This, of course, includes feeding and watering, exercising and giving any medication your pet may require. We/I also spend what we/I call quality time with your pet—just playing, petting and loving so your pet receives personal attention while you're away. We're/I'm happy to keep an eye on your home at the same time by doing such things as bringing in your mail and newspaper, alternating lights, opening and closing curtains and blinds, watering plants—activities that give your home a lived-in look. Our sitters are/I am bonded and insured, and our/my charges are based upon the type of pets you have and the number of visits made. Four days notice is required for our/my services so that we have time to set up an in-home consultation with you and your pet(s). This initial meeting is required before reservations can be confirmed. If you will tell me the type of pets you have and the number of daily visits they will need, I can give you the fee for our/my services.

ANSWERING MACHINES VERSUS PERSONAL ANSWERING SERVICES

Because pet sitting involves making visits to your clients' homes, it will be impossible for you to answer your business telephone at all times. Because you don't want to miss a call, you'll need a reliable way for callers to leave you messages. Your most likely options are to purchase a dependable answering machine or voice mail system, or employ a personal answering service. There are advantages and disadvantages to both of these methods.

First, a personal answering service gives your business just what the name implies, a personal touch. When you can't be by the phone, your calls are forwarded to the answering service you've hired. A person answers your calls and takes messages. Upon returning to your office, you simply call the service and receive your messages. One problem with this method is that the caller who wants to talk to someone right away may be frustrated by reaching a person who can't do anything more than take a message. The phone operators just aren't qualified, authorized or paid to offer specific information about your services. The other negative element is the cost. It is very nice to have calls answered and messages taken, but there's a price involved for this personal service. Shop around if there are several answering services in your community—their prices and services do vary. It's a good idea to check with some of their clients, making sure they are satisfied with the service.

The answering machine has really grown in popularity during recent years. It used to be that everyone hated these machines and refused to leave a message on them. That's changed drastically as people have found that in this busy day and age they just can't function well without them. And our society is becoming accustomed to talking to a machine. Also, the price of this type of technology has come down, making them an affordable convenience in many homes today. Thus, the answering machine or a voice mail system is a viable and very economical means of message-taking for the small business.

When considering this tool for your business, find out what type of voice mail services are available from your local telephone company, independently-owned communications companies and computer soft-ware packages. I know of some pet sitters who installed a computer soft-ware program that gives their callers a menu option, such as press 1 if you would like information about services, press 2 if you're a client who is returning home, press 3 if you would like to receive a brochure and so on. This is an impressive set-up; however, it may be more sophisticated than you really need if you're pet sitting on a small scale.

An advantage of an answering machine or voice mail system is that it allows you to customize or personalize your outgoing greeting messages to fit your business needs; such as holidays, seasons, vacation closings and so on. Some examples of these greetings are shown on page 52. The biggest disadvantage of an answering machine is probably the fact that it can mal-function. Lightning may ruin one during a storm or, unbeknownst to you, your tapes may simply wear out, causing you to lose valuable messages.

Fortunately, these events are few and far between. There is usually little chance of malfunction with a voice mail system, but find out any risks associated with each system when making this important decision for your business. Whichever method you choose, be sure that calls are professionally answered and promptly returned.

> *Note:* The nice thing about a telephone answering machine is the fact that your outgoing message can be changed easily to accommodate your scheduled office hours, seasons or holidays. Because your greeting often creates a first impression of your business, keep it professional. State when callers can expect a return phone call and then meet that expectation. But make your greeting pleasant and interesting, too. If you want to be creative, you can even have a "leave your message after you hear the BARK, MEOW and so on" or have animal sounds playing in the background as you record your greeting.

Sample Answering Machine Messages

Sample Everyday Message

> This is XYZ Pet Sitters' answering machine. Our office hours are from ____ to ____ daily/Monday through Friday (whatever your hours are). If you need information about our service, please leave your name and daytime phone number. If you are a client returning home from a trip, please leave your name and a brief message. Thank you for calling XYZ Pet Sitters.

Sample Holiday Messages

> Happy Holidays! This is XYZ Pet Sitters' answering machine. Our office hours are from ____ to ____ Monday through Friday. If you would like information about our service, please leave your name and phone number where you can be reached during these hours. We are rapidly becoming booked for the holidays, so please make your reservations early to assure service. Thank you for calling.

> Merry Christmas! We're out walking Santa's reindeer now and can't personally take your call—so we hope you'll talk to our machine. We're completely booked for the Christmas holidays

through December 27. Our office is closed until 2 P.M. December 28. We still have a few openings for New Year's and are also taking January reservations at this time. Please leave your name and number after you hear the beep, and we'll return your call between 2 and 5 P.M. on the next business day. Thanks for calling and Happy Holidays.

Sample Message for Inclement Weather

This is XYZ Pet Sitters. Our office is closed due to the inclement weather. For those with reservations, sitters will be making rounds as road conditions permit safe travel. Messages will be monitored, so if you have a cancellation, require information or need to make a reservation, please leave your name and number and we'll return your call as soon as possible. Begin your message after you hear the beep. Thanks for calling.

PAGERS AND CELLULAR PHONES

A wonderful invention that is highly recommended for use by professional pet sitters is a cellular phone. When you consider how handy they are for conducting business from your car (pet sitters often do a lot of driving), they are worth their weight in gold. They allow you to check messages and return calls promptly—plus they provide extra security. Fortunately, their prices have really come down in recent years and there are several calling plans from which to choose; you should be able to find one to fit every budget.

Knowing that help is only a phone call away can be reassuring when you're:

- Walking dogs alone in an unfamiliar neighborhood
- Entering empty homes during evening hours
- Experiencing car trouble
- In need of assistance to locate a missing pet or have a medical emergency
- Running late for an initial client interview

Most pet sitters prefer the small cellular phones that easily fit into their "Survival Bag" or "Pet-Sitting Pak"(a fanny-pack outfitted for pet sitters). These small, lightweight phones can be used while in the car with the cigarette lighter or carried on the body thanks to a rechargeable battery pack.

If cost prohibits you or your pet sitters from investing in a cellular phone, a less costly means of communicating is a personal pager. By wearing a pager, callers can let you know when they need to speak with you. The caller's phone number appears on your pager and it emits a noise, alerting you that someone is trying to reach you. If you, or your pet sitters, don't have a car or cellular phone available, some inconvenience may be experienced as you try to locate a pay phone or delay the return call until you reach your next stop. Still, the pager can be a real time-saver if it prevents you from making an unnecessary visit to the home of a client who has returned early. Some pet sitters tell me that having a pager and being accessible to their clients at all times is a real selling point of their service. They include this point, along with their pager number in Yellow Page advertisements and other promotional material. (Before you do this, however, you'll need to decide if you want to be reachable at all hours of the day or night!) Pagers also come in handy for when clients who need to work overtime want to reach you to arrange a walk for their crated puppy. Some sitters tell me that they have determined an "emergency" code with their spouse or office manager. If that particular code number or word appears across the pager, they know they are needed immediately and need to get to a phone fast.

DETERMINING SERVICE ROUTES

An important part of your preplanning involves deciding where you'll provide pet-sitting services in your community. Initially, you may want to start by working alone and sitting within your neighborhood subdivision, apartment or condominium complex, or within a five-mile radius of your home. This would allow you the opportunity to make sure you enjoy this type of business without incurring the added responsibility of recruiting, training and managing other sitters. If your goal is to pet sit on a small scale (perhaps you have another full-time job or are a stay-at-home mom or dad) for supplemental income, these parameters may be ideal for bringing forth the number of clients that you're able or willing to accommodate.

However, if you are ready for the challenge of a larger staff and service area and feel the demand for pet sitters exists in your community—then go for it! In three years time, I went from two sitters (one being me) to thirty. Obtain a current map of your city or town (often available from the Chamber of Commerce, Town Hall or real estate offices) and then familiarize yourself with it. It is helpful if you are an established member of the community, in which case you are probably familiar with economic boundaries, growth trends, the safer areas and, of course, shortcuts around town. If you are new to the community, pet sitting provides a great way to learn your way around, plus meet many neighbors and area residents.

There are many ways to decide where you'll provide pet-sitting services. You can split your territories into north, south, east, west routes; by zip codes or neighborhoods; by subdivisions or condominium complexes, and so on. Keep in mind the travel involved: if your routes are too extended, your profit may be eaten up in gasoline costs. Define which areas you'll cover and then make sure you're adequately staffed to offer services within them. Also, make sure your advertising defines the areas in which you sit. Otherwise, you'll waste a lot of time answering calls and having to explain that your service doesn't extend to the caller's neighborhood.

SETTING PRICES

Setting prices can be difficult for the new pet sitter because, unfortunately, there's no magic formula for establishing a price structure for your service. There are some guidelines, though, that will assist you as you tackle this important task.

First, do some basic research in your community. Spend some time making brief calls to area boarding kennels, veterinarians, and any other pet-sitting services to see what they charge for keeping various animals. This will tell you what the going rates are for pet care and it will tell you who your competition is. The cost of living in various parts of the country will greatly affect the charges for such services in different regions. Make notes on your findings for comparison and future reference.

Note: Conducting this type of price research is standard in many industries. It is different than the "wannabe pet sitter" discussed in Chapter 1 who poses as a customer and conducts a conversation or participates in an in-home interview in order to gain operating information from existing pet sitters.

Second, decide upon the territories involved for each sitter's service route and the traveling distance rounds will entail. If personal vehicles will be used by sitters, your prices will need to account for gasoline and wear and tear on their vehicles. The simplest way to calculate this is to use the federal government's approved reimbursement per mile which, as of this writing, is 30¢ per mile. If a sitter is responsible for a five-mile radius sitting zone, then the sitter may average around ten miles of travel, or $3.00 in gasoline and wear-and-tear costs. This amount needs to be added to your prices on a per-job basis. A sitter may be caring for only one home and pet and still drive five miles to and from the job. Another time, the sitter may be stopping to care for five customers' homes and pets along the same five-mile route. But, whether it's one stop or five, the same amount of gasoline and wear on the car is involved and so transportation costs should be factored into your fees. By using the government's price per mile, you have something concrete and substantiated on which to base this cost or portion thereof that you include in your fee. If public transportation is used to make service rounds, the cost and time involved will need to be considered when setting your prices.

Note: Another option is to charge separately for gas or transportation costs. I personally find this method complicated and confusing for the client, as well as for the pet sitter! However, if a client is outside of your typical service area you may consider sitting for them with the agreement that they pay an additional amount for mileage based on the government's current approved mileage charge.

Third, time is another important factor to be weighed in establishing your fees. I expected my sitters to spend five to seven minutes getting to a home, a minimum of thirty minutes in the home, and five to seven minutes returning from the assignment or traveling to the next customer's home. This averages out to about forty-five minutes per home. The time and price increase per home if there's more than one pet involved. I also consider the minimum hourly wage and try to make sure the pet sitter gets a reasonable wage for the time, responsibility, risk and occasional inconvenience involved in pet sitting. You'll want your wage to be high enough so the pet-sitter position appeals to the caliber of person you want working for you.

You'll also want to do some calculations to anticipate what the overhead costs of your business will be. After you've gotten estimates on rent, utilities, telephone, printed literature, insurance, bonding, advertising and so on, calculate what you'll need to make on a monthly basis to at least cover these costs, much less pay a salary to yourself and any office help you'll need. To allow you to meet these expenses, you will need to factor into each established fee a flat overhead cost, as well as a margin of profit.

Once you've arrived at your fees, see how they compare with the national average for a pet-sitting visit. This information can be obtained by calling an organization like PSI. Knowing that the prices you charge are within the ballpark of most pet-sitting charges will help you feel more comfortable and confident in setting your fees and in explaining them to your clients.

As of this writing, the national average for a pet-sitting visit is close to $12.00 per visit. Other useful information is that most pet sitters charge by the visit rather than by the day, and most pet sitters charge an additional amount for each extra pet in the home, applying the highest fee applicable and then adding on, for example one dog at $11.00 plus one cat at $2.00 plus one rabbit at $1.00 equals a total pet-sitting visit charge of $14.00. If these pets are visited twice or three times daily, the fee is multiplied accordingly.

Another rule of thumb is that most pet sitters charge a slightly higher fee for dogs than for cats. This is because it usually takes longer to adequately exercise or walk a dog. Others charge the same fee per visit regardless of what type of animal is in the home.

A shortcut method to setting prices is to survey what your area kennels are charging for overnight stays, and then add $2.00 to $5.00, according to your transportation and overhead expenses, for a per visit fee. If a client only has one pet, then a pet sitter will usually be more expensive than a kennel. Keep in mind though, that if it's a multiple-pet owning household, a pet sitter is usually less or comparable to a boarding kennel.

Some pet-sitting services offer a senior citizens' discount (usually 5 or 10 percent) to encourage business from those fifty-five and older. A few firms offer a 10-percent discount on monthly contracts or assignments involving ten days or more. They consider this discount to be an incentive for pet owners who are taking long trips. One pet sitter I know offers a 10-percent discount to all clients whose cats or dogs have been spayed or neutered. Firmly believing in spaying/neutering as the solution to the pet overpopulation problem, she sees this discount as a way of encouraging the procedure and rewarding those who participate in it.

If the final figure(s) for your price structure seems high to you at first, remember this is a personalized and professional service you'll be providing. Don't undersell yourself or the valuable services offered by a professional pet sitter. After all, you're making it much easier for a pet owner to leave home with peace of mind. On the other hand, be realistic in setting your prices—don't price yourself out of reach. Although you can go up or down on your prices, setting your fees and sticking to them will create credibility and give you a more professional image, so it's crucial for you to do your homework. Some trial and error may be involved, and your public will quickly let you know if you're too high or too low. Put forth the effort required to be on the mark and competitively priced.

Should you find yourself competing with other pet sitters whose prices are lower because they are not insured and bonded or they don't operate in a professional manner, don't be discouraged or dissuaded about your fees. My experience has shown that quality always wins out and that people get what they pay for. Unfortunately, there are some who quickly go into pet sitting without giving it the proper forethought required. They soon find their prices are too low for them to make any money and quickly become disillusioned, and usually don't last too long in the business. When confronted with the client who tells you that "Such and such a service only charges X dollars for a visit," tactfully reply "Well, they know what they are worth." Just because someone is cheaper doesn't mean that they're better!

Note: Whenever possible, it is best to adhere to your price structure. However, there will be times when you may increase a fee or offer a discount. Occasionally, someone may book services who lives two doors away or across the street from you or the assigned sitter. With no gasoline or great distance involved in the job, you may feel a smaller fee is appropriate, or your sitter may request a lowered rate for the customer. On the other hand, a customer may have more than what's deemed normal in houseplants (a greenhouse for example) that will need watering. If what's needed in a home requires more than the average amount of time you have calculated in your fees, then, of course, you'll raise your fees accordingly. However, a litter of kittens that are still feeding from their mother may not require any additional efforts of a pet sitter, so you should not treat them as additional cats in your sitting fees. Most of your calls will involve routine pets and the typical care that is included in your established fees. Whenever there is a question, I always try to give the customer a minimum and maximum figure for services. I then allow the sitter to make the final determination about fees after seeing what the job entails.

HOLIDAY FEES

In the past, many of us thought that working on holidays was simply a part of the job when it came to pet sitting. After all, it's not the customer's or pet's fault that the pet needs care every day of the year! Thus, some of us thought that it was not fair to charge extra for visits made on Christmas Day, Easter Sunday and so on. A new trend of charging extra for holiday visits is becoming more commonplace within the industry. Just as a plumber or doctor or other professional would charge more for a holiday visit, some pet sitters are charging an extra $5.00 per visit for rounds made on federally recognized holidays. Many firms give the entire surcharge to the assigned pet sitter as a means of compensating him at a higher rate for working on holidays. Some firms split the additional charge with the sitter involved.

The idea does have merit and the practice does command professional respect for our industry; however, you'll need to decide what your policy will be. I wanted to charge extra for holidays but when I put the question, along with a vote, to my staff sitters, they vetoed it to my surprise. The consensus was that it unfairly penalized the client and might put our services out of reach for some regular customers who weren't used to a holiday surcharge. And because most of our customers showered the pet sitters with holiday gifts, goodies and/or tips, some said they were afraid the clients would stop this practice if holiday fees were increased. Although I never was able to implement this policy in my business, it is something to carefully consider. Higher pay would certainly make those holiday visits easier to make when you'd rather be home or celebrating with family and friends!

Note: Holidays are always busy times for professional pet sitters. Therefore, careful planning is a must. The owner of a very large pet-sitting service told me that she sends out a postcard one month before Thanksgiving that states she is holding a holiday reservation for the customer for the next 72 hours. To confirm the reservation, the client must remit a non-refundable deposit within this 72-hour period. If the early reservation is not confirmed and the client calls later, he or she will have to take their chances that a pet sitter will be available. This system helps the office manager to preplan for holiday staffing needs. Whatever your system for handling these peak periods, just be sure to double-check all reservations with your pet sitters to make sure no pet-sitting visits are overlooked!

COMPENSATING SITTERS

When setting the pay rate or commission splits for sitters working in your organization, keep in mind the overhead costs, along with the profit you want the business to realize. You'll need to be fair, though, in compensating your staff members. Their time, travel and work are extremely important to your reputation and success. Although the work is usually very enjoyable, few pet lovers can afford to do it for nominal pay. Set a competitive pay scale that motivates sitters to take pride and do a good job as representatives of your company.

Some pet-sitting services pay by the assignment and others pay on an hourly basis; some start sitters at what amounts to 40 percent of the total charges, others pay good sitters as much as 60 percent of the fee charged to the client. Although there is no set pay scale, there are rules relating to whether you're utilizing pet sitters as employees (typically paid by the hour) or as independent contractors (typically paid on a commission basis or by assignment). Talk with a good accountant for sound advice regarding compensation rates and methods. Make sure that what you pay is enough to attract the kind of dependable and trustworthy sitters your business needs.

HANDLING CUSTOMER COMPLAINTS

If you have done a good job recruiting pet sitters and tracking their performance with rating forms or telephone follow-ups, you should have few, if any, complaints. Regardless of how terrific your service is, however, sooner or later you're bound to run into the customer who lives to complain. Or perhaps there will be a legitimate problem, and the customer will be justified in criticizing your service or sitter. To help you manage such confrontation, I have outlined the way I handled the few complaints that were lodged against my pet-sitting business:

- I always listened open-mindedly to what the customer had to say. Believing in the people who sit for my organization, I conveyed to the customer my surprise and concern about the complaint.

- I next expressed my sincere regret about the complaint and asked for the opportunity to discuss the problem with the sitter involved, believing that there are two sides to every story.

- I assured the client I would be back in touch with him or her promptly and thanked the client for bringing this concern to my attention.

- I then reached the sitter involved as quickly as possible and attempted to get to the bottom of the complaint. If, after hearing both sides of a story, I thought the sitter was in error, I apologized profusely to the client and waived or reduced payment for services rendered. In two situations, I contacted our insurance company to file a claim for the damages incurred by the client (and was thankful I had good insurance in place!).

If I thought the complaint was not justified, I explained to the client the sitter's and business's stand or defense in the matter, and that I hoped he or she understood our viewpoint or action. I came to realize that there are some people you can never please and that we were better off without their business. Fortunately, I found these people to be few and far between! Again, knowing your sitters helps in these instances. You probably won't know most of your customers, but if you have spent time interviewing and screening your pet sitters, you'll be more confident in believing, trusting and defending their actions. In addition, keep written evaluations from your clients on each pet sitter to help you feel good about (and be able to defend, as necessary) the people working on your behalf. It's extremely important to recruit and hire only those individuals who will be assets to your business. Excellent sitters are the key to no complaints and to the success of your service.

> *Note:* It's important to have your sitters make you aware of any problems they encounter on a sitting assignment. This way you'll be better informed and better able to address a complaint. Better still is for you or your sitter to call the customer and explain a situation before it becomes a complaint. The daily notes to a client left by a sitter are also used in explaining problems and how they were handled, which can prevent a complaint. And when discussing problems, I believe honesty is always the best policy.

"ALWAYS READY" SERVICE

One of the highest compliments you can receive as a pet sitter is when a customer asks you to permanently keep a house key on file. This means she is pleased with your service and plans to use you regularly. It is repeat business like this that helps your business be successful. Not only does being asked to permanently keep a customer's key mean she likes and trusts you, it also decreases the amount of time you (and your customer) will have to spend picking up and returning house keys. However, there is increased responsibility and liability involved when you permanently retain house keys. You'll want a formal system in place that encourages clients to become regular clients and that permits you to keep the keys organized and secure while in your possession.

The program I developed for my pet-sitting service was called "Ready-Key." We promoted it as a convenience to busy clients who often had to travel spontaneously for business or as a time-saving program for frequent travelers who didn't want the inconvenience of meeting us for key exchange. Although we usually required a minimum of four days notice to pet sit, we were often able to accommodate Ready-Key customers on shorter notice because we knew their pets and routines and already had house keys on file. It was not uncommon to never see our Ready-Key customers after the initial interview consultation and first sitting assignment. They simply made reservations by telephone, their sitter made the requested pet-care visits, and the client either left payment on the kitchen counter for the sitter or mailed it in upon returning home. It was a great arrangement for all concerned!

To sign up for the Ready-Key program, I had forms printed that stated the customer was authorizing my company to keep two (2) house keys on file (one for our office and one in the possession of the assigned sitter) so that pet care visits could be made with minimal notice. By keeping a key in the office, we were assured access to it and to the client's home if the regular sitter should be unavailable due to a scheduled vacation, illness or emergency. (Accidents do happen, so obtaining two sets of house keys is an ethically sound business practice.) The client was charged a nominal $5.00 to enroll in the program, which helped cover our program administration expense.

Each enrollment form was then coded with a number that was also attached to the customer's house key. An index card was also used to record the client's name and Ready-Key code number. The enrollment forms were then filed alphabetically by customer name. The index cards were filed in another secure place by code numbers. The coded house keys were maintained in a locked key cabinet. Thus, only my office manager and I knew where each of the files was stored. In the event that my office was ever burglarized, it would not be easy to match up house keys with addresses!

Fortunately, a burglary never occurred and our Ready-Key program became very popular with customers. We even received a couple of calls from Ready-Key customers who had locked themselves out of their homes. Calling their pet sitter to let them inside was less expensive than calling a locksmith!

PLANNING FOR DISASTERS

When I first started pet sitting, the worst calamity I could anticipate for my new business was the possibility of snow and ice during the winter months that would make travel hazardous—or impossible. What would I do if I could not safely get to the pets in my care? While running my business, we not only experienced bad snow and ice storms, we also had a hurricane and tornado wreak havoc in the community. Both incidents were very unusual weather but both caused quite a bit of damage and problems in making pet-sitting visits. These experiences showed me the importance of planning for such events. By having a plan in place, you'll be able to stay calm and take appropriate actions for the well-being of your business and the pets in your care.

Because almost every area is susceptible to some type of disaster, such as snow, ice, hurricanes, tornadoes, floods, fires and so on, obtain the name and phone number of a neighbor or someone within walking distance of your client's home who also has a key to the home; then, should fallen trees or hazardous driving conditions make it impossible for you to visit a home, at least you'll know someone to contact who may be able to get to the home to check on the animal(s). This back-up procedure would only be used in case of extreme emergency, and your client should be made aware of this. And, for sitting reservations during months typically known for hurricanes or snowstorms, it's a good idea to request that your customers make such arrangements with neighbors; let them know that you would only call in the event of an emergency. Or, in the event of a hurricane, the customer may request that the pet(s) be evacuated and taken to a kennel or veterinarian's office for safekeeping. If this becomes necessary, you'll need to know where the pet carriers can be found along with supplies to be transported for the pet. Time can be of the essence, and you don't want to waste time looking for pet carriers that may not exist!

Put some thought and research into preplanning for disasters now. Talk with local professionals and contact such organizations as the National Humane Society for any information they have on disaster preparedness for animals. Find out if your local humane society has a volunteer with a four-wheel drive who would assist you or your pet sitters in getting to homes during a snowstorm. Compile your findings into a formal written plan for your business operations during such events. You'll be glad that you have such a reference available should it be needed—and your clients will be impressed that you have a plan in place!

CLIENT INTERVIEWS AND CLIENT PRESENTATION BOOKS

The purpose of an initial client interview is twofold. You want the client to have the opportunity to meet you, or the assigned pet sitter, so they will feel more comfortable with the person to whom they may be entrusting the care of their pet and home. You (or your sitter) need this time to get acquainted with the pet, and to personally be shown the pet's routine and household layout by the customer. A professional pet sitter should always insist upon this initial meeting before accepting an assignment. You should also let the client know that the reservation is not guaranteed until this introductory meeting has taken place and a service contract has been signed by the client and pet sitter.

Note: Sometimes family emergencies make it impossible for initial client interviews to take place (for example, the pet owner must leave immediately as the death of a relative is imminent). However, be cautious when accepting assignments when you haven't met the pet (or

client) in advance. Get as much information as you can by phone and emphasize to the customer that this is an exception to your normal operating procedure. I did find that the customers with emergencies whom I was able to help on short notice were extremely appreciative and often became repeat customers.

Here are a few tips regarding client interviews:

- Allow thirty to forty-five minutes for each interview.
- Remember that first impressions are important. Keep a change of clothes or shirt in your car if you'll be conducting an interview after or in between pet-sitting visits where you might get covered with pet hair or muddy paw prints. A comb or brush through the hair is advisable if you've been outside walking dogs. Although you don't want to wear a business suit to an interview, neither do you want to look like something the dog dragged in.
- Client interviews are business calls, not social hours. Be friendly, courteous and professional as you lead the meeting. Try to conduct it at a dining room or kitchen table rather than leisurely sitting on a living room sofa. Refrain from accepting a cup of coffee or snack—especially if you're on a tight schedule!
- The client will be watching to see how you interact and react to his or her pet(s). Give the pet time to get used to you before making friendly overtures.
- Obtain good written instructions and notes about the care of the pet(s) and home.

- Be knowledgeable and prepared to discuss any company policies, such as payments, late night visits, insurance carrier and so on.

If all goes well and a service contract is filled out and signed, assure the customer that he or she is in good hands and that you look forward to working with the animal(s). Many pet sitters use what is known as a "Client Book" in conducting initial customer interviews. The "Client Book" is a loose-leaf notebook or scrapbook in which they've included the following items:

- A business brochure or business card
- Copy of their city/county business license
- Copies of any credentials, such as education diplomas or certificates, memberships in trade organizations, Chamber of Commerce, Better Business Bureau and so on
- Certificate of liability insurance and dishonesty bond
- Photos of their own pet(s)
- References from pet-sitting customers
- Photos of other clients' pets
- Sample of their service contract
- Business cards from pet sitters around the country or from local pet-sitting networks (clients are impressed at the size and professionalism of our industry and are reassured by the camaraderie and networking that often takes place among pet sitters—get business cards from other pet sitters at local meetings or national conventions)

The "Client Book" allows you to make a professional presentation of your pet-sitting service that is impressive to the customer. It also permits you to lead the interview and keep it on track. If the relationship is determined to be a good one between the pet, pet sitter and client, then a service contract can be completed and house key exchanged before the initial meeting concludes.

Some pet sitters charge for this initial meeting just like it is a pet-sitting visit and others charge but apply the fee towards the first contract if services are used. Others, like myself, don't charge because we see the initial interview as much for our benefit as for the customers'. We prefer to think of the time spent as an initial investment in the future of our businesses. There is no right or wrong way here but again, it is a decision that you'll have to make for your pet-sitting service.

USING A COMPUTER

The office procedures described earlier in this chapter worked well for me and enabled me to efficiently operate my business for many years. However, as my business and customer base grew, my husband convinced me that a computer would be a laborsaving and timesaving addition to my office. About three years into the business, I reluctantly purchased a computer and a letter-quality printer. My husband was right (as usual), and I quickly found that a computer can be used in myriad ways. Here are just a few of them:

- Maintaining a mailing list for any business correspondence, advertising or newsletters
- Building a customer data base
- Tracking the advertising methods you use
- Tracking delinquent accounts
- Bookkeeping chores
- Printing lists of reservations by day, week, month or sitter
- Keeping up with sitter birthdays, anniversaries and even birthdays of clients' pets!
- Tracking company growth by zip code area

And much, much more. I know a few pet sitters who have purchased software that contains a map of their city service areas. They are able to actually pinpoint client addresses and map out a route for daily pet-sitting visits! A computer is also great for helping you produce a client newsletter.

In earlier editions of this book, I said that a computer is not an essential piece of equipment for a pet-sitting business. This is still true if you're in the beginning stages or if you want to remain a small-scale service (less than 50 clients). But because computers are so prevalent today, there's probably a good chance you already own one. If so, by all means, use it in your business. If you don't already own one, I wouldn't consider this a vital purchase until you're established and committed to growing your business. Managed growth will be a much easier task when you have computer options available.

CHAPTER 4

PERSONNEL

FINDING AND QUALIFYING PET SITTERS

The most critical factor to your success is the selection of the pet sitters who join your organization. You know your own abilities and that you will do a wonderful job of pet sitting, but you have to be absolutely sure you find the right people to help you. There is much at stake in this business of caring for other people's pets and homes, so recruiting personnel is an area that deserves careful thought and consideration.

What do you look for in potential pet sitters? My experience has shown they need to be:

- True pet lovers
- Dependable and reliable
- Trustworthy individuals
- Able to provide their own transportation and telephone
- Comfortable and happy meeting the public

With these criteria in mind, you might try approaching your friends, family and neighbors to ask if they can think of anyone to recruit. Chances are one of them will volunteer to help, and you will have your first employee! Be sure to explain, however, that this will be a business relationship with no special privileges.

If possible, try to find sitters who come highly recommended from someone whose opinion you trust. If you do not know applicants, learn as much about them as you can. Other excellent sources of pet sitters are local kennel clubs, cat clubs and humane societies. Possibly some of their members will be interested in pet sitting or will know of others who would be good candidates. Either call or write to these groups, explaining your service and need for additional pet sitters. The following is the letter I've used for this purpose:

Humane Society, Kennel Club Letter

Dear Humane Society Members:

Enclosed you will find information explaining our new pet-sitting business, XYZ Pet Sitters, Inc. Our service is available to pet owners in the city and the surrounding areas. We would appreciate it if you would announce our service at your next meeting.

We also wish to support your organization. Please send us information regarding membership at your earliest convenience.

Our service area covers a large territory and as our business grows, we plan to enroll the services of many more sitters. If your organization has anyone or knows anyone interested in working in their neighborhood area to care for pets, we would appreciate your referring them to us.

We thank you for your time and look forward to serving you and your pets in the near future!

Sincerely,

XYZ Pet Sitters

Another good method for finding qualified staff members is to check veterinarians' offices, especially those located within the area in which you need additional help. Often veterinary technicians or office workers will be interested in pet sitting as a second source of income. With their veterinary hospital experience and an employer's recommendation, such people will most likely be good pet sitters.

When you've exhausted your sources of personal referrals, you may find that you'll need to advertise in your local newspaper under "Help

Wanted." I remember being very uneasy at first about using this method. Fortunately, my worries were unfounded, and I had some very nice individuals apply for our openings. Of course, there were a few less-than-desirable applicants, but I found my instincts useful in weeding these people out. I knew the type of person I was looking for to represent my business, and I could almost immediately tell if a candidate held promise. With time and practice, you'll develop these skills as well. The following are some samples of ads I used in recruitment.

Sample Help-Wanted Ads

> Perfect Part-Time Job!
> Must Be Honest, Dependable,
> Love Animals, Have Car and Enjoy
> Public. Flexible Hours.
> Serious Inquiries Call:
> XYZ Pet Sitters
> 999-8877
> March 3 and 4 from 2–4 P.M.

> XYZ PET SITTERS has openings in your neighborhood area! For info., call 999-8877 March 3 and 4, 2–4 P.M.

> PET LOVERS!
> Perfect part-time job. XYZ Pet Sitters, Inc. has openings in southwest, northwest & southeast areas of W-S/Forsyth Co. Have fun and earn money caring for pets in your neighborhood. Must be at least 21 yrs., have exc. refs., love pets, have transp. & be available 7–9 A.M. and 5–7 P.M. daily. Serious inquiries call 999-8877, 3–5 P.M. Mon., Jan. 11 & Tues., Jan. 12.

Regardless of how you find your pet sitters and how well you know them, always have job seekers complete application forms. It is best if they return forms to you directly so you can discuss the position with them. Review applications while the applicant is there to answer any questions you may have and to get better acquainted. If after their initial interviews you feel they are well suited to be pet sitters, your next step is to check references thoroughly.

Note: I know of a few business owners who require that each person answering a newspaper ad submit a resume. The rationale here is that if the person is professional and interested enough in your opening, he or she will willingly and promptly mail credentials to you. If the person isn't willing to meet this request, he or she is immediately disqualified. This is a good way to distinguish the good candidates from the bad and saves you interviewing time. Regarding the all-important screening process, I required at least two personal and business letters of reference before permitting any candidates to join my company as pet sitters. (No matter how well I knew them, policy is policy, and it's best to allow no exceptions to the rule.)

You should also discuss screening applicants with the insurance agent who sells you your bond. Through experience with bonds, he or she may have required applications or suggestions to help you find trustworthy individuals for your organization. Before checking references on an applicant, make sure you have his or her written permission. Many companies will not release information about a former employee without a signed authorization to do so. There are some business owners in large metropolitan areas who conduct a very thorough investigation of each potential pet sitter. Besides the personal and business references, they check the applicant's driving record, credit history, and they ascertain that the applicant has no criminal record. Some business owners look these records up themselves, while others require that the applicant produce these records or hire a data collection service to conduct the various searches. Regardless of the checking methods you use, make every effort to learn as much about your applicants as possible. Due to the nature of pet sitting and the risks and liability involved, you need to feel very comfortable and confident about the character and abilities of your staff members.

Note: Many business owners are finding it to be faster and more thorough to use the services of a background screening company when checking references. These companies can check records in multiple states and submit their findings to you in writing for your records. Today, you can't be too careful about the people you hire to work for you, so a professional background-checking company can help simplify this process. Clients are impressed to learn that you go to such lengths. Check your local Yellow Pages for "Employee Background Checks," or call PSI for recommendations.

Another requirement I had of my sitters is that they be at least twenty-one years old. By this age, people usually have a couple of years of work or college experience that add to their common sense and maturity. Customers seem to have more peace of mind in having an adult look after their pets and home than, for example, a high school student.

Although it was not intentional, all but seven of over a hundred trained sitters I've worked with over the years were female! I find this interesting. As mentioned earlier, this trend continues with approximately 91 percent of U.S. pet-sitting firms being female owned and operated. Perhaps the flexible schedule or nurturing aspect of pet sitting appeals more to women, and customers seem to feel more at ease handing over their house key to a female sitter. You may find this to be true for your business as well.

I have found that pet sitting appeals to teachers, nurses and graduate students as an extra source of income with flexible hours. I've also had several married couples, two mother and daughter teams, and sisters who worked for my company. These sitting duos were extremely popular with our clientele. Evidently customers like the double dose of attention their pets receive from a team visit! I also had several real estate agents come on board as pet sitters. The flexible hours worked well with their schedules and permitted them to earn additional money. Your clients can also be an excellent source of pet sitters. I've obtained some of my best sitters this way. They used our service, were extremely pleased and then called to see if we had job openings. I had such good luck with clients who became sitters that, whenever we needed additional sitters, I advertised in our client newsletter, and I kept an ongoing list of customers who indicated their interest in pet sitting if an opening became available.

Retirees and senior citizens also make great sitters. In addition to enjoying the pets, many love the activity and public contact that pet sitting provides. Many are affectionately known as "grandma" or "gramps" to their colleagues and clients! I know of several senior citizens who have built their pet-sitting businesses into manageable businesses that provide nice supplemental income, and they can fit in a game of golf between morning and early evening pet-sitting visits!

There are lots of great people out there who will do a first-rate job of pet sitting for you, so don't be nervous when it's time to expand your staff and to delegate more sitting assignments. It is likely that you'll have more applicants for pet-sitting positions than you have openings. Don't forget professional courtesy once you've found your new pet sitters. It's my opinion that if someone has taken the time to complete an employment application and talk with you, the least you can do is mail a letter of explanation or rejection. Applicants are grateful for the notification, and this attention to detail speaks well for your company.

APPLICANT INTERVIEWS

The personal interview is all-important during the recruitment process. Keep in mind that this person may be going on client interviews for your company. Make a note of the following impressions:

- Was the applicant prompt for your interview?
- Was the applicant appropriately groomed and dressed for your meeting?
- What was the applicant's demeanor during the interview— friendly and interested or nervous and ill-at-ease?
- Would you feel comfortable opening your door and allowing this person into your home on a first-impression basis only?

During the interview, you'll want to go over the position requirements and get more in-depth answers to questions asked on your application form. If the applicant works another part-time position, find out the hours involved and if they will conflict with your position requirements. Have the applicant elaborate about ownership of pets, present and past. Ask questions to draw out the applicant in conversation. This will help you evaluate his or her speaking skills, intelligence and personality.

Although I always conducted interviews at my place of business, I know of some pet sitters who prefer to interview at restaurants. They say this allows them to assess the applicant's table manners and comfort level in a public setting—plus, it allows them a lunch or dinner as a business expense! Other pet sitters prefer to conduct an initial interview at the applicant's home. This allows them to see, among other things, how tidy the applicant is along with the type of pet(s) owned by the applicant. They think they get to know the applicant better after seeing them on their own turf. Yet other pet sitters insist that the initial interview be held in their own homes. This setting allows them to imagine the applicant as if he or she was making an initial visit to a customer's home. How the applicant interacts with the owner's pets is an important part of the evaluation process!

Become familiar with labor laws so that you are not discriminatory in your hiring practices. Contact the Department of Labor or local office of the Wage and Hour Administration for current laws affecting employers.

SITTER ORIENTATION

Whether it's one new pet sitter or an entire group, it's very important to train your sitters in an orientation session. You'll want them to understand your company's policies, procedures and what you expect from them as members of your staff. The more informed your pet sitters are, the better job they'll do as representatives of your company.

Attendance at an orientation session before your new pet sitter takes on any assignments should be mandatory. After this session, many of my pet sitters told me they had no idea so much was involved in being a professional pet sitter. They were amazed and appreciative of all the information conveyed during our training session. They were also surprised at the length of the session: from four to six hours, depending upon the number of questions raised and amount of discussion. To help you conduct your own training sessions, below is an overview of what took place in mine. This is only a suggestion of possible format and content. Depending on your geographic location and climate, there may be some specialized services your company will want to provide (for example, pool cleaning) in addition to the more general services provided by a pet sitter. The basics follow and you can tailor your own orientation to fit your business.

I began each session with introductions and then handed out folders of supplies (service contracts, business brochures and cards, notepads, key tags, self-addressed envelopes and so on) that the pet sitters would use when working. I next explained that the purpose of our training session was not to scare new pet sitters with all the things that could go wrong in the course of business, but, instead to prepare them to avoid any problems and know how to handle them should they arise. I wanted my sitters to always be thinking and using their common sense.

After presenting some history on our company and the pet-sitting industry itself, I discussed certain company formalities, along with policies and procedures, that included the following:

- Compensation—when and how much the sitter is paid
- Insurance coverage—the kind our company carried

I next showed a training video I produced, "The New Pet Sitter." The video takes a new sitter step-by-step through an actual pet-sitting visit. The video is a great training tool, not only because it's effective, but also because it allows the presenter to take a break and rest his or her voice for a few minutes. I highly recommend that you incorporate the video into your orientation session (see the Addenda for ordering information). If it's not a possibility for you at this point, you can easily explain the ins and outs of pet sitting to your staff.

During this session, there are some points you should stress to new pet sitters:

- Emphasize the importance of confidentiality of customers' names. You never know who may overhear your conversation as you describe the gorgeous art, coin or gun collection in the Smiths' home. Customers' names and the contents of their homes should remain confidential; letting their absence be known could invite a burglary. Coding house keys anonymously is also important in the event that keys are ever lost or stolen. I instructed my sitters to code them by visit or stop (for example, 1, 2, 3 and so on). That way, only the sitter knew to which house the key belonged. Make your customers aware of their anonymity; this gives them peace of mind while they are away.

- An introductory meeting with the client and his or her pets is an absolute must, unless extenuating circumstances preclude it. This is normally a thirty to forty-five minute visit that allows the client time to fill out your service contract and gives the sitter a chance to become acquainted with the pets and their routine. The meeting helps ensure that a client feels comfortable because he or she knows the person who will have responsibility for his or her pet and home. Likewise, it also ensures that the sitter knows that the assignment is one he or she feels comfortable accepting. It's an eerie feeling walking into a stranger's home and dealing with a pet you've never met before. All in all, an initial interview is highly recommended.

- Returning clients' house keys can be handled in different ways. Some customers prefer the key left in their home on the final visit. Others want it held by the sitter and returned in person, just in case the owner is not able to return when planned. Many people these days have dead-bolt locks for which a key is necessary to lock the door; therefore the key has to be returned in person. (In such cases, you may want to charge extra for the sitter's time and gasoline in returning the key, unless you've already allowed for this when setting your fees.) Many of our regular customers signed up for the "Ready-Key" program discussed in the previous chapter so that our services would be on call as needed. This is nice as it shows your services are well liked and also cuts down on time and gasoline usage in key pickups. In any event, you'll need to inform your new pet sitters of the various modes of key return, unless your company has a single procedure for this.

- Undoubtedly you have put thought and research into setting fees for your pet-sitting services. Thoroughly explain your pricing during orientation and spell out what the customer receives for this fee. Although you or whoever answers your business phone will usually quote prices for services, sitters should understand how to calculate fees and be able to respond intelligently to routine inquiries about prices.

- Discuss your company's payment policy. Will clients pay their sitter directly and trust that payment will be forwarded to the company, or will clients mail payment to your office? Will major credit cards be accepted and, if so, how will this be handled? Are sitters allowed to accept tips and if so, must they report them for proper taxation by your company? And do they keep the entire tip, or split it with the company? This is an important area that requires serious attention so as to avoid any confusion or misunderstanding.

> *Note:* Speaking of tips, inform new sitters not to be surprised at customers who remember their pet sitter with a souvenir or gift from their travels. Point out how good you feel to make rounds to a home during holidays and find a Christmas gift or Valentine's box of candy for *you* from "Muffin" or "Snowball" or "Fluffy." These thoughtful little remembrances from customers can make your day. Also, I know of one pet sitter who stamps her service contracts with "100 percent of gratuities go directly to your pet sitter." This not only tells the client that tips are accepted, but it also lets them know that they go directly to the pet sitter. Since implementing this idea, she told me tips from clients had really increased and of course, her sitters were thrilled!

- Because driving is such an important aspect of pet sitting, stress to your sitters the need for careful driving habits at all times. The last thing you want is a speed demon representing your organization. Also, a clean car speaks well for the integrity of your pet sitters.

Note: For your own peace of mind, you may want to obtain an umbrella automobile insurance rider for your business. (This coverage was mentioned in Chapter 2 under "Insurance" but deserves repeating.) If one of your sitters has an automobile accident while pet sitting and expenses exceed the limitations of his or her car insurance, your business policy would afford additional coverage. Discuss this with your insurance agent.

- Go over any equipment or supplies you require or recommend during pet sitting. I remember when I first opened my pet-sitting business, I tried to think of *everything* I might possibly need in the course of pet sitting. I bought so much—paper towels, garbage bags, pooper scoopers, flashlight, whisk broom and so on—that I had to carry a huge bag to make rounds. What I quickly learned was that people who have pets have the items necessary to do a good job caring for their pets. The initial items I suggested my sitters invest in included the following:

  - A clipboard to hold service contracts so the customer has a hard surface to press on when filling it out. While the customer completes the contract during the initial interview, the sitter is free to get acquainted with the pets in the household.

  - A key retriever of some type is absolutely mandatory, whether it's a string tied around a wrist or a belt clip-on type. There is nothing more horrifying than to have the wind blow the door shut (and locked) while the sitter is outside with the pet, and the key is on the kitchen counter. This is not only embarrassing, but it can be time-consuming and expensive if a locksmith is required to get the sitter back into the house. So, stress to your sitters the importance of keeping house keys attached to their bodies while making pet-sitting rounds. I have tried all types of key retrievers and find the elasticized plastic wrist bands are preferred by me and my sitters.

  - A city map is helpful for shortcuts and finding streets when you thought you knew where you were going.

  - A schedule book, whether it's a date book or simply a monthly calendar, is absolutely necessary for keeping up with pet-sitting visits, initial interview appointments and staff meetings, not to mention all the other things one may need to remember in this busy day and age. Write it down so you don't find yourself needing to be in two places at the same time.

- A flashlight can be very useful when pet sitting. It can help you let yourself into a dark home, find an elusive cat that hides in nooks and crannies and serve as a weapon if need be (the battery-filled handle can pack a powerful punch should you ever need to defend yourself with it).

- A leash because although clients should always provide one to use for walking their dogs, sometimes they forget to leave it where you can find it. Or, a worn leash could break from the strain of an energetic dog. Having a back-up leash may prove handy.

- Flea repellent is a necessity for the occasional home that's filled with fleas. You don't want to carry the fleas into the home of another client or back to your own home. Nor do you want to be "eaten alive" while caring for the household pets. So invest in a good flea repellent.

- Discuss the type of notice you'll expect from sitters for vacation, illness and even resignation. You will need advance warning to schedule assignments and guarantee services to clients. Requiring a week's notice from sitters is reasonable; sitters usually know of upcoming vacations, engagements or exams. Of course, you can never plan on the flu, so in the event of a sitter's illness, have a back-up plan, or you'll find yourself scrambling at the last minute to feed hungry pets.

> *Note:* If you'll be hiring pet sitters as employees, you may want to require that they sign a non-compete clause prior to joining your company. This would prohibit your employees from taking your customers and starting a competing business for a certain period of time after leaving your employment. Discuss this with your attorney—a non-compete form or clause is a legal contract. You'll need legal assistance in preparing a document that will protect you in your state.

- Insist that your sitters recognize and take advantage of free advertising at every opportunity. Advertising is expensive and sometimes beyond the reach of the small business—yet it's vital to any new business. There are many ways to spread the word about your services, though, with little or no expense. Ask sitters always to carry business cards and/or brochures and post them on bulletin boards in public places. Leave these items in a variety of business establishments and hand them out at social and civic gatherings. When shopping, give business cards to salesclerks. Give thought to places and people you may not have considered before; even those who may not have a pet probably know people who do and who may need your services. Word of mouth is often the best form of advertising for a service business, so implore your pet sitters to spread the word about the pet-sitting services your company provides.

- Suggest that your sitters study literature from your office library or visit the local public library to familiarize themselves with the various types and breeds of dogs, cats and other household pets. A client will always be impressed when a pet sitter is knowledgeable about his or her particular pet.

- Tell your sitters the name of your insurance company and your agent's name. Discuss with them what your insurance covers, stressing the need for their conscientiousness while pet sitting.

I gave each of my sitters a letterhead form, signed by my insurance agent, that briefly stated and explained the types of insurance coverage carried by my business. This was proof of our coverage should a customer ever request it.

> *Note:* A representative of the insurance agency that administers the group liability policy for pet sitters spoke recently at an annual convention. He stated that the primary reasons pet sitters were filing claims on their insurance were because of the following:
>
> • Doors being left open! Animals get out and are hit by a car, run away or bite someone. Or, animals get into a home via an open door and damage the interior.
> • Dogs get loose while being walked and either run away, bite someone or are hit by a car.
> • Water damage! Either from watering plants and having dripping water damage furniture or from leaving a faucet running that causes flooding in the home.
>
> These instances account for more than 80 percent of the claims filed by pet sitters, and the first is the reason for more than 50 percent of the claims. Share this information during orientation sessions and stress to new sitters that they need to be especially cautious when opening exterior doors, walking dogs, watering plants or running water in the home.

• A true sign of a conscientious, professional pet sitter is a daily note or log left in the customer's home. This may state the time of the visit, how the sitter found the pets and home upon each visit, weather conditions and so on. I furnish "daily diaries" for this but insist that a note be left on whatever paper is available. Customers have raved about these notes and have said they enjoyed reading them very much. The daily record gave them assurance the sitter was there and made them feel as if they hadn't really been away. Some sitters are brief in their notations and others write essays on the antics of the pets. The notes come in handy should a customer return early and wonder if the sitter has already fed the pet(s) that day. Also, if a pet acts peculiarly, the sitter can make daily notes to cue the owner in to a potential problem. If a problem has occurred, the sitter can explain in the daily note what has transpired. Otherwise, the customer may wonder what took place in his or her absence. The daily notes are a very important part of your service. If pet sitters are doing a good job, the customer should not be able to tell the sitter has been around—except for the daily note.

- You'll want to know if customers are pleased with your services. A good way to get feedback is to have sitters leave some kind of evaluation form. Discuss the importance of this form with your new sitters. You or your sitter may also want to provide a self-addressed envelope with the evaluation form to encourage customers to return the form (and their payment!) to you. A rating form gives you valuable information based on customers' comments, suggestions and even constructive criticism. You can also use it to find out how they heard about your services to assess what form of advertising is working for your business.

- Returning customer calls promptly is a must for you and your sitters in creating a professional, positive image for your business. If it takes three days to return a call, a customer may wonder if

your delivery of services is also haphazard. Even if customers are not leaving town for several weeks, they still appreciate speaking with their sitter and knowing they can count on the prompt, professional services of this individual. After talking with their sitter and being assured of services, customers are relieved and feel secure in making flight or travel reservations. So always insist sitters call and introduce themselves to their customers as soon as possible—and preferably within twenty-four hours of the client's call to book pet-sitting services.

- First appearances do make strong impressions on people, so remind your sitters of this and request that they be neat and clean when going to an initial interview. To project a professional image, sitters should not smoke, chew gum or accept an alcoholic beverage while pet sitting. Smoking can plant the fear of a house fire in customers, while accepting an alcoholic beverage can create concerns about raids on their liquor cabinet. So, even though pet sitting is very informal, it is best to forego any of these activities because they reflect negatively on your professional image. Besides, the duration of house visits for interviews and service rounds is not *that* lengthy. Insist that your pet sitters refrain from smoking, drinking alcohol or gum chewing while on duty.

- Taking the garbage out on a final visit to a customer's home is a nice touch and speaks well for the thoroughness of your services. Empty cans of pet food in the trash tend to smell as they accumulate. Depositing the trash in an outside container results in a more

pleasant return for your customer. If your customer is away for an extended length of time, the sitter may need to take the trash out more often.

- Advise new pet sitters never to let a client leave a key hidden outside for them. Clients are notorious for leaving town in a hurry and forgetting this all-important task. An extra key can be made for a very small charge and given to the pet sitter, but a locksmith can be expensive, not to mention the extra time this will entail. Also, don't agree to let clients drop their house keys in the pet sitter's mailbox. Mail carriers have been known to pick up these keys (or envelopes with keys in them) and assume they are to be conveyed through the postal system.

- If pet sitters are to leave a self-addressed envelope for the client (to pay your bill and/or return your evaluation form), encourage them to provide business-sized envelopes. Clients don't like to fold their checks or forms origami-style to fit small envelopes!

- If a sitter learns about the death of a client's pet, he or she should let your office know. Then you can change your records accordingly and send a sympathy card or remembrance to the customer.

- Remind new pet sitters that feces should always be disposed of in a sanitary manner. Insist that the client or sitter provide plastic bags for this phase of cleanup.

- Tell sitters to always try contacting their absent clients should a disaster occur in your area. If there is an earthquake, tornado or hurricane, clients will most likely hear of it through the media and worry about the safety of their home and pets. The sitter should call the client promptly and give as much information as possible.

  Note: If you have developed a formal disaster plan for your service, you should discuss it and recommended operating procedures with new sitters. Be sure to copyright it before distributing copies to personnel.

- If you've not already mailed a brochure to a new client describing your services, request that your sitters leave one during their initial meeting. The fact that you have printed literature creates a more professional image for your business, so take advantage of it.

- By requiring a certain amount of notice from clients prior to their departure, you should have ample time to arrange for an initial interview with their sitter. However, clients will have emergencies due to illness or death and need to leave immediately, without meeting the pet sitter. Discuss these emergency situations with new pet sitters and your company's policy in handling them.

- Spend some time discussing how emergency pet-sitting situations should be handled. Should sitters contact you at home, call another staff member or handle the problem as they see fit? Prepare your new pet sitters with a plan of action for emergencies so that they won't panic should one occur.

- Get emergency numbers from your new sitters. If a sitter becomes sick or injured while pet sitting, you'll need to know whom to notify. Or should you be unsuccessful in contacting one of your staff members, you may need to check with this emergency contact to ascertain the well-being and whereabouts of your pet sitter.

- More than likely, the insurance and bond coverage you purchase for your business will only cover sitters themselves in the course of performing pet-sitting duties. Stress to your sitters that for this reason, among others, they should go *alone* when making pet-sitting rounds. The customer has authorized only the sitter or your company's representative to have access to his or her home and pets. Should an adult friend or family member accompany a sitter and even sit in the car, neighbors may be watching and later exaggerate the scene by describing "a carload of people" who showed up to care for the pets. To avoid any unnecessary problems, the sitter should always work alone. If a sitter requires assistance with an assignment, then you will need to intervene, making the client aware of any problems and the reason additional people were needed to enter his or her home.

- Furnish pet identification tags that state the name of your company and business phone number. Instruct new sitters to place one on each dog or cat having access to the outdoors for which they will be sitting. If the pet becomes lost (after darting out the front door when the pet sitter is entering!), anyone finding the pet will know whom to call. See the Addenda for ordering information.

I'm being cared for
by XYZ Pet Sitters, Inc.
999-8877

- A final word of advice you could offer is to encourage your new pet sitters to conduct business by the Golden Rule. Treating each customer, pet and home as they would their own will surely minimize the potential for problems and help pave their path to success.

The next part of my orientation and training session for sitters involved going over the various literature and business forms my service used. These items were placed in the information packets mentioned at the beginning of this chapter. Although some of the forms were self-explanatory, I still reviewed each one. I wanted to make sure new pet sitters understood the reason for each piece of printed material and that they knew how and when to use it. Because you'll want your new pet sitters to be thoroughly informed, I suggest you devote some time to form and literature explanation in your training sessions.

Although pet sitters are not expected to be roving veterinarians, a good pet sitter should be able to recognize the symptoms of illness in a pet and have some knowledge of first aid if a pet becomes injured or sick while under your company's care. I know of a few pet-sitting services that require their new pet sitters to volunteer several hours at a local veterinarian's office, thereby gaining valuable experience in dealing with sick or injured animals. The American Red Cross has recently started teaching a course in pet first aid. Check to see if this class is available in your area. If so, it would be an excellent training program for professional pet sitters.

Another way of approaching first aid in your training sessions is to show videos that deal with the subject. Although these were not available when I first began to expand my staff, there are now a few good ones on the market. There are also interesting videos available on the proper care of rabbits, ferrets, various types of birds and reptiles, along with cat care and dog breed identification. Most videos and pet books are reasonably priced, so consider providing an office library of first-aid and pet-care books and videos that new sitters may borrow. Given the low cost of some of the books, you might give each new pet sitter a paperback book on general first aid for pets, or you could require that sitters purchase a copy as an integral part of their supplies.

After a final question-and-answer period, I concluded my training sessions with a pop quiz. This was a multiple choice test that included questions from all the areas addressed in our orientation. The test allowed me to see which new pet sitters had a complete understanding of what pet sitting involved and what our company policies and procedures were. By the test scores, I could see which areas needed further clarification or which attendee had slept through the training program. (Anyone napping during the session would be immediately disqualified from joining our staff; however, I'm glad to say this never occurred!) An additional benefit of the test was that clients were always impressed when they learned that my pet sitters were not only trained, but they were tested as well. Thoroughness in training heightens the level of professionalism and increases credibility. Make every effort to get your new pet sitters off on the right track. This initial training will pay off in the long run.

SITTER SAFETY

Professional pet sitters, like real estate agents and pizza delivery personnel (there's that pizza analogy again!), are at risk because they go into strangers' homes for interviews, enter empty homes during pet-sitting visits and walk dogs or exercise pets outside at all hours of the day and evening. Thus, pet sitters should not be naive or complacent about personal safety. Incorporating some discussion of this issue into your orientation session is highly recommended. Stress to your sitters that this subject is not meant to scare or deter them from pet sitting, but merely to increase their awareness of an important subject. As the saying goes, an ounce of prevention is worth a pound of cure! The following are some safety tips I've gathered from my years in pet sitting:

- Be alert. When you feel uncomfortable in a situation, get out of it.
- Keep your photograph and those of other pet sitters on file in an easily accessible place in your office. Also keep car models and license numbers, driver's license numbers, whom to contact in cases of emergency and any important medical information. (Consider having each new pet sitter write down this information on an index card during orientation and then clip it to a Polaroid picture you take of each sitter before the session ends.)
- Report any suspicious experiences to local law enforcement right away.
- Develop a coded distress signal with your office personnel, pet sitters and/or your family. This would permit the person in danger to call the office or home with a message that sounds innocent but would alert others that something is wrong and help is needed.
- If uncomfortable at an initial meeting with a client, say that "a back-up sitter" (or spouse) will be showing up at a property at any time as

it is usual company policy for two people to know the location of every customer's home and pets in case of an emergency.

- Dress conservatively for initial interview meetings with customers.

- Don't carry a pocketbook while pet sitting. Instead, keep identification and necessary items on your body in a "fanny-pack." And leave the jewelry at home!

- Carry a personal alarm or shrill whistle and don't hesitate to make as much noise as possible if you feel threatened. Yelling "fire" or "911" alerts others to an emergency.

- Make sure you know beforehand who else (and what type of car they may be driving) has access to the customer's home.

- Never allow anyone else (other than those authorized in writing by your customer) into the client's home.

- Familiarize yourself with the areas in which you provide sitting services. Know safe routes for dog walking, the location of police/fire departments, stores with late hours and so on.

- Keep your car in good running condition with your gas tank filled. Remember to lock your car doors while driving and while parked at client homes.

- Other than your staff or family members, keep absent pet owners' names and travel dates confidential.

- Leave an outside light on (or ask clients to use timers) so that evening pet-care visits don't have to be made in the dark.

- Have house or car keys in hand and ready to use when arriving/departing during your pet-sitting rounds.

- Carry a cellular phone with you while pet sitting.

The following are more helpful tips from various pet sitters on the subject of sitter safety:

- Make noise upon entering an empty home. If a burglar is inside, he may run the other way. If the client or a family member is there, he or she won't be surprised by your appearance!

- The initial client interview should tell you what the animals, customer and home are like—don't take the job if you are uncomfortable with any of these!

- Lock the door behind you when entering a client's home.

- Always call the dog's name before entering, and turn down the job if the dog is aggressive or has ever bitten anyone.

- Personalize the home by positioning an item in the house; if it's removed or disturbed, you'll be alerted that undesirable activity may have taken place.

- Advise a friend or spouse of when, where and for how long you're meeting a customer along with contact information. I ask a friend to call my cellular phone during the meeting so I can alert her (through a secretly understood code phrase) if I'm concerned about my safety. So far I haven't had to use this phrase! Immediately upon leaving the home, I call to let her know all is well and profusely thank her.

- Check with your local police department for any booklets they have available on home and personal security.

- Share pertinent tips with customers.

- Do a complete outdoor security check of the house before entering, making sure doors and windows haven't been broken into or tampered with. Be aware of your surroundings, indoors and outdoors; a forced door or missing items means leave and call police immediately.

- Ask pet sitters to call and report the time of arrival and departure at each client's home. Call your own answering machine with updates of time, where you are and where you're headed for visits.

- Carry mace or pepper spray with you but make sure you know how to use it. Also, consider taking martial arts or a self-defense class.

- Don't accept jobs in unsafe neighborhoods, and take someone with you for evening visits.

    Note: Be sure you have the customer's permission, in writing, to enter the home with someone else.

- Ask someone to accompany you if you ever feel uneasy about making a visit.

- Wear reflectors on your shoes and clothing so cars can see you at night.

- Remember that the dog you're walking can be a warning system. Pay attention if the tail stops wagging or ears stand up!
- Have a rehearsed plan in your mind so that if you're attacked while walking a dog, you know exactly where your whistle/personal alarm/pepper spray is or what you will start screaming.
- Know two exits for each client's home.
- Park in well-lighted areas, when possible, and always lock your car doors while making pet-sitting visits.

   Note: Thanks to the members of Pet Sitters International who contributed the above suggestions for personal safety while pet sitting—you know who you are! It is imparting ideas like these that helps our industry as a whole and that makes membership in a professional society so beneficial and valuable.

SITTER NUTRITION

This new subject for this edition of my book shows how far pet sitting has come. In the "old days" when I, and pet sitting, were much younger, we never gave a thought to something like "Sitter Nutrition." We were so glad to be working and pet sitting for people that eating—much less eating correctly—was the least of our worries! Now, with the public emphasis on eating healthily, pet sitters have expressed concern at

Feline Food Pyramid

national, regional and local meetings about how to do this with the hectic schedules they sometimes face.

With careful planning, you don't have to sacrifice nutrition just because you're working during normal meal times! Here are some suggestions that would be helpful to share with staff members, especially at orientation sessions for new pet sitters:

- Because pet sitters are known to frequent fast food places, order grilled or sliced meats, not breaded or fried.
- Try a low-fat muffin or bagel for breakfast.
- Order a small hamburger instead of a deluxe, or super; better yet, order a salad.
- Use catsup, mustard or vinegar instead of mayonnaise.

Plan ahead for meals or hunger pains by carrying these foods with you:

- Low-fat snack crackers, pretzels or popcorn
- Fresh fruit
- Homemade soups or stews—in thermos containers or ask clients for permission to use their microwave ovens
- Canned fruit, tuna or chicken in pop-top cans
- Fruit juices
- Low-fat breakfast bars, fig bars or drinks
- Veggies—easy to carry in a small cooler
- Graham crackers or low-fat cookies
- Low-fat potato chips or nacho chips
- Dried fruits; raisins, apricots, dates and so on
- Lots of water
- Protein bars
- Bites of cheese (in a cooler)
- A healthy sandwich (in a cooler bag with ice)
- Containers of cottage cheese or yogurt available in a cooler

Eating "on the run" does take planning but doing so can result in a healthier diet as well as maximum use of time spent in the car at traffic lights or during rush hours. Suggest that your new sitters give serious thought to this because most pet-sitting rounds are made during break-fast, lunch or dinner hours! Remind them, too, of the calories they will be burning while walking and exercising pets!

SURVIVAL ITEMS

In addition to the recommended pet-sitting supplies previously discussed, there are a few more items that I, and many of my colleagues, have found to be helpful in the course of pet sitting. Most professional pet sitters purchase a canvas bag or fanny-pack that is referred to as the "Pet Sitter's Survival Bag." This bag is kept in vehicles or another convenient place so it can easily be thrown over the shoulder before heading out to make pet-sitting visits. Items kept in the Survival Bag include: paper towels (why are there usually only two on a roll at a client's home?!), rubber gloves, can opener, hooded rain slicker (for unexpected downpours!), WD40 (for temperamental house keys!), pet toys, pet first-aid kit, human first-aid kit, tissues, snacks, personal grooming items (comb, brush, makeup and so on), squirt bottle or gun filled with water and lemon juice or vinegar (can be used to divert stray dogs that try to approach you when walking a dog), identification and spare change. Other supplies such as a clipboard and business literature can also be carried in this bag. If you come up with other recommended items for "survival" as a professional pet sitter, please write to me at the address included for Pet Sitters International in the Addenda. I'd like to share your ideas with readers in future editions of this book.

MANAGING AND MOTIVATING SITTERS

Starting your own pet-sitting service may present you with your first experience managing employees, and you may need some assistance or reassurance in this area. First, remember that a pet-sitting business is some-what non-traditional compared to other business environments. After you've recruited and trained your staff members, you'll probably find that you communicate mainly by phone and rarely see them. That's why I feel that pet sitting is one of the few businesses that still thrives on the old-fashioned element of trust. There must be trust between the client and the pet sitter, as there must be trust between the pet sitter and the employer. You won't be able to follow your pet sitters and check on the jobs they do for you; you'll have to trust that they will satisfactorily fulfill their job obligations. You will also need to trust that clients will let you know if they are displeased with your company's services.

That's why it's important to use some type of client evaluation form or to call your clients for feedback about your sitters and services; then share this information with your sitters. If they are doing a terrific job, tell them, praise them, commend them! Let them know how much you appreciate their efforts. Likewise, if there's any type of complaint or dissatisfaction, constructively discuss this with the sitter; then put your discussion and the outcome of it in writing and file it in the sitter's personnel file. Should the same complaint be voiced again about the pet sitter, you'll have good docu-mentation for supporting whatever disciplinary action you decide to take.

Hopefully, if you've gone to the trouble of finding good pet sitters, you'll be singing their praises instead of disciplining them.

Note: Because you'll be seeing your staff members infrequently, consider taking or requesting their photos for display on your office bulletin board. This allows you or your office staff to put faces with names and personalizes your operations a little more. You'll also be able to give a physical description of the pet sitter for identification if requested to do so by a client. And, as discussed in the previous section on "Sitter Safety," this is a wise practice.

Pet sitting is different from more traditional businesses in that it usually requires part-time or "split-shift" employees who work on call, with usually no guaranteed paycheck and minimal, if any, benefits. The work can be demanding, with weekends and holidays often the busiest times and, as with any job, you need to be on guard against burn-out. To do this, make sure your pet sitters have an occasional weekend or holiday off. Keep enough pet sitters on staff or back-ups available so that you're not too dependent on any one sitter. If you started your pet-sitting business by making all the visits yourself, remember what some of the jobs and some of the clients can be like—and be considerate of your staff members! If you're good to your employees, they'll be good to you.

Experience has shown that most people who want to be pet sitters do so because of a genuine love of animals and the appealing nature of the flexible work hours and independent work. It has been said that nursing or teaching takes a special kind of person, and I've found this to be true of pet sitting as well. But, as in any profession, some inspiration is nice and necessary to keep these "naturals" motivated and eager to do a good job for your company. The following are some ways to motivate your pet sitters:

- Institute a sliding scale of compensation. In other words, give your pet sitters some economic incentive! Give small pay increases after every three or six months of service with your company, or whatever your budget can handle and you feel comfortable with.

- Hold sitter contests. Give prizes or cash awards for the sitter who sits for the most clients each month, brings in the most new business each quarter, or receives the best evaluation forms from clients each month.

- Give a yearly Christmas or "appreciation" bonus to sitters who've done an outstanding job during the year. Sometimes the gesture and recognition means more to employees than the actual amount of the bonus.

- Send out monthly letters to staff members. Tell them of any new business policies or procedures. Inform them of any discounts on services you're now offering. Introduce new staff members. Commend pet sitters who've done an exemplary job. Announce winners of contests. Use the letters to keep sitters informed and motivated. (A sample letter appears after this list.)
- Charge a holiday surcharge for visits (discussed in Chapter 3) made on certain nationally recognized holidays. Give the surcharge to the pet sitter as a bonus for working during holiday periods.
- Give pet sitters reduced fees on pet-sitting services from your company.
- Try to arrange a discount for your employees at an area pet store or with a local groomer as a company benefit.
- Remember employee birthdays and company anniversaries with a card and/or small gift.

- Use photos of employees in your advertising—they will love the publicity and notoriety!

- Recognize sitters who have made a suggestion that increased revenues, improved morale or operating procedures and so on. This can be done in monthly sitter letters, in client newsletters and during staff meetings.

- Celebrate National Professional Pet Sitters' Week (the first full week of March each year) by holding a luncheon for employees or placing an ad in your local newspaper that thanks your hard-working pet sitters.

- Nominate deserving pet sitters for the prestigious "Pet Sitter of the Year" Award sponsored by Pet Sitters International.

Sample Monthly Sitter Letter

April 1, 1997

Dear XYZ Pet Sitters:

Thank you, thank you, thank you for helping us survive a March that had the flu making the rounds! Many thanks to those who provided substitute sitting services and to those who assisted in taking last-minute reservations for the Easter weekend period. The clients you helped have really expressed their gratefulness and assured me they will be using us again soon!

There are a few things you need to be aware of. Our T-shirt order will arrive April 25. Please make plans to stop by the office to pick up your "summer uniform." These should be great for the upcoming warm weather months!

The luncheon held at The Red Onion Bistro on March 6 in recognition of National Professional Pet Sitters Week was a lot of fun and well-attended. You guys are just the greatest and as I expressed at the luncheon, I really appreciate the terrific job you do as XYZ Pet Sitters!

The Triad Veterinary Emergency Clinic has moved into larger quarters. They are now located at 924 Maple Boulevard, near the I-40 exit ramp. Please make a note of their address—the phone number is the same!

Don't miss this rising star! The daughter of our own Joann Hampton is starring in the Little Theatre's production of "Annie" in the leading role. The play will run April 28–May 14.

continues

Our "Sitter of the Month" is a pet sitter who obviously enjoys her work and is always willing to go the extra mile, according to the client evaluations this office has received! Congratulations Pam Johnson! Keep those eyes and ears open for "running toilets" and coffee pots left on—your customers sure appreciate (and for good reason!) your attentiveness to their homes. Your gift certificate to Oak Valley Mall is enclosed. Enjoy some shopping on XYZ Pet Sitters and know how proud we are to have you on staff!

Sitters celebrating birthdays this month include Donna Boren (2nd), Bob Williams (8th) and Betsy McGillicutty (24th). Hope each of you will have a very happy day!

It is with much sadness that we must say good-bye this month to a special pet sitter who has worked with us for three and a half years. Debora Leonard, we and your many customers (two-legged and four-legged) are sure going to miss you. But we wish you and your husband, Andy, much luck and happiness with your relocation to the Washington, D.C. area. Please stay in touch!

Because the busy summer months are fast approaching, please let the office know as soon as possible of any dates when you will not be available for sitting assignments. We're receiving many calls already for summer reservations!

Until next month, happy pet sitting!

STAFF MEETINGS

Regularly held staff meetings are important to keep your staff informed and can be good motivators. They allow you to personally interact and communicate, and they allow your sitters the opportunity to meet each other and compare sitting experiences and knowledge. I always tried to make my meetings educational as well by inviting a guest speaker to talk about something that would be helpful to my staff members. We had presentations from veterinarians, pet photographers, kennel club spokespeople, humane society personnel and tax accountants. Our local agricultural extension agent gave an informative talk on the care of houseplants and our local police demonstrated self-protection techniques. During one get-together we watched a dog first-aid video, and at another we addressed postcards about our services for a direct mail campaign. Several sitters got to know each other well from these meetings and became good friends. The meetings provided a sense of community and the camaraderie was always enjoyable. The refreshments I provided were a way of thanking the sitters for their dedication and good work.

Consider having these meetings as your budget allows. Hold them in your home and make them potluck if nothing else! It's the sharing of information that will count and benefit your sitters. Plus, it's impressive to clients when they learn that these meetings are held on a regular basis and that education is on-going for your staff members.

Note: When a pet sitter leaves your organization, it's wise to notify clients for whom they have worked that they are no longer with your organization. It is best to do this in writing. This would release you from any liability should the former pet sitter continue to pet sit for the customer.

EMPLOYEES VERSUS INDEPENDENT CONTRACTORS

Your legal relationship with your staff is an extremely important decision that you'll need to make. Will the pet sitters who work with you be treated as employees or will you utilize independent contractors for pet care services? This is truly one area where you'll be wise to consult with an accountant and an attorney. The Internal Revenue Service is supposedly taking a hard look at all industries using independent contractors. Those businesses that are audited and found to have employees instead of independent contractors can incur severe monetary penalties. Learn all that you can about what constitutes an employee and what is accepted by the IRS as an independent contractor so you can make an informed decision for your business's personnel needs.

Currently the IRS uses a "20 Question" test in assessing whether someone is working as an employee or independent contractor. Request this pamphlet from the IRS if you're entertaining the idea of using independent contractors. It will help you to more knowledgeably discuss the issue with accounting and legal professionals. The early trend in the pet-sitting industry was to use independent contractors due to the sometimes seasonal nature of the business and because of the savings in taxes and paperwork the practice provided. Now, with pet sitting growing in prominence and profits, many business owners are going the employee route so they will have total control of their business and so they don't have to worry about an IRS audit! Because I am not an accountant or an attorney, I will not try to advise you in this area other than to say do seek good professional counsel on this facet of your business!

CHAPTER 5

ADVERTISING

THE MEANS TO THE MASSES

Your office is organized, your staff trained, your insurance and bond are in effect and you're ready to begin pet sitting. How do you get that phone ringing with customers requesting your services? You have to get the word out about your business and seize every opportunity you can to educate the public about the valuable in-home pet care you provide.

Advertising is a critical factor in the success of your business. After all, people won't patronize your business if they don't know it exists. I made a mistake in advertising when I opened my pet-sitting business in 1983. I began my business on such a shoestring budget that there was little left over for advertising. Had I spent more on my initial advertising and reached more people, I'm sure my business would have grown much faster. There is much to be said for the old adage that you have to spend money to make money. So, when planning your operating budget, be sure to allot an adequate figure for advertising, especially during your first few years of operation.

Knowing your goals for your business will help you determine your advertising campaign. If you're planning to pet sit to earn some extra spending money, then putting out doorknob hangers on homes in your immediate neighborhood area and perhaps running an ad in your neighborhood newsletter will be the only advertising you need to do. However, if your goal is to run a large pet-sitting service that covers the entire city and/ or county in which you live, you may consider grand opening ads in the local newspaper and spots on a local radio or television station. Advertising costs usually increase according to the number of people you want to reach.

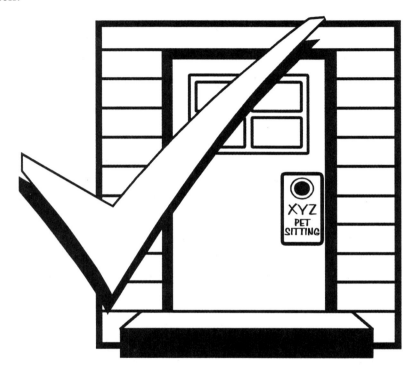

As you might expect, the usual mass-appeal forms of advertising (television, radio, magazine, newspaper and billboard) can be overwhelmingly expensive for the small business just getting started. However, through many years of experience, I've discovered there are many ways to advertise your pet-sitting service that can be very effective and involve only a minimal cost. I'll discuss these inexpensive advertising techniques first— a penny saved is a penny earned.

THE IMPORTANCE OF A BROCHURE

To start, have a nicely printed brochure describing your pet-sitting service. Your brochures and business cards will come in handy time and time

VACATION TRAVEL??

You can trust your pet to us.

XYZ Pet Sitters, Inc.

- personalized, loving in-home pet care

- make your home look "lived in"

- reasonable rates

- four (4) days notice required

- service available in 27103, 27104, 27106 areas of Winston-Salem

Since 1983
Winston-Salem, NC
999-8877

XYZ Pet Sitters, Inc.

— Bonded —   — Insured —

again in promoting your service. Often, they'll create the first impression of your business so it's important that these materials be well-written, attractive and indicative of your professionalism.

If graphic design is not your area of expertise, hire someone in this field to help you create this literature for your service. There are many freelance designers who may do a good job but charge less than an established advertising or public relations agency. Again, interview prospective candidates for experience and credentials, and shop around for the best deal.

A good brochure should contain information about what your service provides, the advantages it offers, how it works and probably, how much it costs. You may also want to include some background material about yourself and/or your pet sitters, relating why you started the business, your past experience, and the number of pets in your own household. You'll definitely want your company logo and phone number prominently displayed, and you may want to include a photo of yourself and/or your staff members on the brochure. Although there will be an initial expense in the writing and layout of your brochure, it will be money well spent. You'll then have a nice brochure representing your business that you can use proudly for years to come.

> *Note:* An added bonus to a well-designed brochure is that you can often take just the front section of the brochure or a particular portion of it and have it enlarged for use as a flyer or small poster. Keep this idea in mind when preparing your business literature to get the most mileage out of your advertising budget.

A word of caution about using photographs of people: Although they add a personal touch (prospective customers like to see to whom they may be giving a key to their home!), photographs will increase your printing costs and can date a piece of literature. You, or your subjects, should dress generically so the photo will look current with today's styles and fashions. However, when you have a dog under one arm and a cat under another, very little of your clothing will show! Because employees do come and go, it is probably best to picture yourself, as the business owner, on your brochure.

A WORD ABOUT "LICENSING"

Of course, you'll want to advertise that you are insured and bonded on your business literature as these are important selling features of your service. However, please don't follow the practice of some pet sitters who list the term "licensed" as a business credential. As of this writing, there is no such thing as licensing for professional pet sitters. Electricians, real estate agents and hair dressers have to be licensed by the state, but to date this is not true for pet sitters.

The use of the term "licensed" indicates, to most people, that criteria have been met usually requiring study and an examination. When a pet sitter lists the term on a brochure, business card or advertisement, the reference is to the fact that the proper city, county or home business license or permits have been obtained. Although these type of licenses do indicate that one is running a legally established enterprise, they mean nothing as to the skills or education of the pet-sitting professional.

I believe it is misleading to the general public for pet sitters to use "licensed" as if it were a business credential, rather than a form of city or county taxation. I'm not sure how the practice began, but most likely a pet sitter innocently began advertising his business license and then a competitor felt compelled to use the wording and the practice snowballed and became commonplace in some areas. Because pet sitting involves a lot of old-fashioned honesty, trustworthiness and ethics, I think pet sitters would be wise not to misrepresent what the term "licensed" means to the industry.

A much more meaningful credential is the accreditation program for pet sitters that has been created by Pet Sitters International. These are home study courses that allow a pet sitter to achieve designations of Pet Sitting Technician, Advanced Pet Sitting Technician, Accredited Pet Sitting Service and Master Professional Pet Sitter. Although the government may step in one day with regulations for the pet-sitting industry, these educational programs are our own attempt at self-regulation. And because each program level does require a course of study and satisfactory completion of an examination, the term "accredited" is much more impressive, and truthful, to the general public.

BROCHURE AND BUSINESS CARD USES

Once you have your brochures, flyers and business cards, the following are some ways they can be used to advertise your services:

- *Grooming shops and pet stores.* Go where the pets are and introduce yourself to the management. Ask for a moment of their time to explain your pet-sitting service and then ask if you may leave your brochures and business cards in a conspicuous location.

    Note: Businesses will be much more receptive to displaying your business cards or brochures if they are presented in a plastic or cardboard stand (available at office-supply or pet-sitting supply companies). Be sure to tape a business card to the back of the stand. This will identify to whom the stand belongs and will serve as a permanent display of your name and phone number should all the cards or brochures be taken. Check your displays regularly to make sure they are well-filled with literature!

Try to develop harmonious relationships with other pet-related businesses. A reciprocal working relationship can be advantageous. Find out if pet stores produce a client newsletter in which you might advertise, or ask if the pet store is willing to give you and your pet sitters merchandise discounts in exchange for a free ad in your company newsletter. Discuss the possibility of holding a spring or fall "pet fair" at the pet store (for further details, see Chapter 6, "Public Relations").

- *Veterinary offices and boarding kennels.* Send a letter of introduction that asks for a personal meeting; then follow up by phone to arrange a mutually convenient appointment time. Don't be afraid to approach veterinarians who offer boarding facilities for pets or kennel owners. Although you are each other's competition, hopefully, you can establish a harmonious relationship. There will be times when boarding facilities will be completely booked or a vet feels that an older pet should be left at home, and the veterinarian may refer customers to you. Likewise, there may be a time when you are completely booked or feel a pet needs more medical attention than you are comfortable providing.

Extending the hand of friendship should be an easy task for today's new pet sitter. The industry has become sufficiently established so that the boarding industry realizes pet sitters are here to stay and that there are advantages to working together. I've even had several kennel owners attend my pet-sitting seminars who told me they realized at-home pet care was the trend of the future so they were adding it to their existing operation in order to be a more full-service business. I, and other pet sitters, have also had veterinarians tell us they were glad we were providing at-home pet-care services. They explained they actually believed it was better for pets to remain in a familiar, comfortable environment and only boarded because there had not been an alternative for pet owners previously. They said they much preferred to keep their limited boarding spaces available for pets that required medical care. Although every vet or kennel owner may not greet you with open arms, I think you'll find the majority receptive to your friendly overtures.

> *A word of advice, though:* If you sincerely want to build a good relationship with boarding industry members, do not engage in negative advertising. Don't depict a dog behind bars on your brochure as if that is what going to a kennel is like, and don't use

the phrase "kennel cough" as stereotypical of a kennel. It's hard to win friends when you're referring negatively to them. Several kennel owners have shared with me that they are offended and insulted when such tactics are used by pet sitters. It is much more professional to advertise the positive features of at-home pet care and enjoy good rapport with other pet-care professionals. After all, some pets do well and enjoy being boarded; others are happier in the home environment. With 60 percent of American households owning some type of pet, there is enough business out there for everyone! Establishing a cooperative relationship with local veterinarians and boarding kennels can be very beneficial for all concerned, including the pets and their owners. It also speaks well for your professional maturity.

- *Travel agencies.* Visit or write all the travel agencies in your community informing them of your services. Supply them with your brochures and business cards. A trifold brochure fits neatly into the jacket of an airline ticket! Consider offering each travel agent an incentive (coupons redeemable for your services or even $5.00 per customer who uses your services). Another idea is to offer clients of the travel agent a special introductory fee on the use of your services. Travel agents often do a lot of traveling—plus, they can certainly connect you with the traveling public! The following is a sample letter of introduction.

Travel Agency Letter

Dear Employees of Vacation Travel Agency:

Enclosed is information describing our personalized home pet-care service, XYZ Pet Sitters, Inc. We would appreciate it if you would circulate or post our brochure in your office. Our service may make traveling much easier for many of your clients!

We are happy to provide you with additional brochures upon request. We look forward to serving you and your customers and appreciate any referrals.

Sincerely yours,

XYZ Pet Sitters

Sample Promotion Letter

XYZ Pet Sitters, Inc.
123 Any Where Street
Any Town, USA 22002
Telephone 999-8877

During the months of April, May and June, XYZ Pet Sitters, Inc., is having a special promotional campaign for travel agents. Since 1983, we have been providing the best in personalized home pet care to residents faced with traveling. In an effort to increase our business, we are offering the following promotion to local travel agents because you know best who may be in need of our services.

- A $5 commission to each new customer you refer to us who books our services for a minimum of three visits. This $5 referral fee will be paid the first of each month (May, June and July) directly to the agent responsible for sending the client to us.

- A 10-percent introductory discount will be extended to your clients who use our services as a result of your referral (new clients only).

Brochures describing our services and discount coupons (which the referring agent will sign) will be provided by XYZ Pet Sitters, Inc., for your use during this campaign. The brochures will easily fit inside the jackets of airline tickets, business envelopes and so on. Your participation could include asking your clients if they have pets that will need to be cared for, or simply inserting literature about our services in your mailers. You determine how actively you participate in our promotional campaign.

I hope you will take part in the promotion—we can all benefit from it. Your agents can earn extra money, your clients will appreciate the discount extended through your agency, and our list of satisfied customers will grow.

Please call us at 999-8877 by April 3, 1997 if you want to participate in this campaign and we'll get brochures and coupons to you promptly. I look forward to working with you this spring!

Very truly yours,

Patti J. Moran
President

Coupon

XYZ Pet Sitters, Inc.

XYZ Pet Sitters, Inc., is pleased to extend a 10-percent introductory discount to the clients of _____. This coupon must be presented when a house key is picked up by XYZ Pet Sitters, Inc., and is valid only for services consisting of three of more visits per home.

Expires 12/31/97

Travel Agent

- *Humane Society, kennel clubs and cat associations.* Write to these organizations, enclosing your brochures and business cards. Offer a free pet-sitting visit to anyone adopting a pet through your local Humane Society, or offer kennel club members an introductory discount on their first use of your services. These are important groups to notify about your business; the chances are great that individuals associated with them are true animal lovers who most likely will need your service at some time. The sample body of a notification letter is shown in Chapter 4, "Personnel."

- *Newcomers to your area.* These are people you continually want to reach because they probably don't know their neighbors well enough to ask them to look after their pets. "Home" is probably somewhere else, so many newcomers will most likely travel for holidays. How do you reach them? Write to your local Chamber of Commerce informing the organization about your business (or consider joining the Chamber of Commerce if the benefits of membership are worth the annual membership dues). Contact your local welcome wagon, newcomers' club or similar groups with information on your services. Mail your brochure to all the real estate agencies in your community. They sell homes to newcomers every day! Also, a growing service in many communities makes moving easy by seeing that utilities are hooked up and turned on for newcomers. If such a service exists in your area, ask the people if they would tell newcomers with pets about your business. I know of one pet sitter who learns about newcomers by checking the water connections, which are public city records. Regardless of how you find newcomers, don't miss out on the business they can provide. And once you've determined who they are, try sending them a welcoming letter that, of course, introduces your service such as the following:

Newcomer Letter

Dear Newcomer:

Welcome to your new home! We hope you will enjoy our city and all it has to offer. As lifelong residents of the area, we can truly say this is a great place to live and work. We hope you'll soon agree!

In the event that you are a pet owner or a potential pet owner, we want to make you aware of XYZ Pet Sitters, Inc. We find that new residents face a problem with what to do with their pets when traveling on business or pleasure. Often, there is no family close by to call on, and neighbors take a while to get to know. In any event, we want to make you aware of our service and hope you'll take the time to read the enclosed brochure, which explains our business in more detail. You can rest assured that each staff member is bonded and insured.

Again, welcome to the area. Please call us if we may be of service to you.

Sincerely,

XYZ Pet Sitters, Inc.

Real Estate Company Letter

Dear Employees of ABC Realtors:

Enclosed is our brochure describing our services to the community. I think we may be of service to you while you are taking vacations, business trips or working overtime. Your pet-owning clients may also find our services of special interest. We would appreciate it if you could circulate or post our brochure in your company.

Please keep our service in mind as you sell real estate to newcomers in our area who are pet owners. We would be happy to furnish you with additional brochures upon request.

Thank you for your time and consideration.

Sincerely,

XYZ Pet Sitters, Inc.

- *House-cleaning and lawn-care services.* Using the Yellow Pages, write to all of these types of services with information about your pet-sitting business. The people doing this type of work visit homes every day; they notice pets and can spread word of your services or leave a brochure for their clients. You could also ask if they would include your brochure with their next billing, or if they would rent their mailing list to you. You may have to offer something (money, discounts, reciprocal referrals) in return for this help in advertising your business. But some may remember what it was like when they started out and sympathetically give your service a plug!

- *Garden clubs.* Obtain a list of the garden clubs in your service area and write to them, enclosing your brochure. Even if club members don't have pets, they probably have plants that need water and care when they're away from home. Remember that anyone who hears about your service may tell someone else, creating a grapevine effect. This is how you can inexpensively get the word out that you're in business. The following is a sample of this type of letter:

Garden Club Sample Letter

Dear Maple Leaf Garden Club:

Enclosed you will find brochures describing services provided by XYZ Pet Sitters, Inc. Although our primary function is personalized home pet care while the owner is away, we also are happy to provide loving care for your plants. Prices are based on travel and time involved; however, we are reasonable!

We are a locally owned and operated business, and we are bonded and insured. We would appreciate so much your announcing our service at your next club meeting. We hope we may be of service to your members in the near future.

Sincerely yours,

XYZ Pet Sitters

- *Law enforcement agencies.* It is a smart business practice to inform your local police and sheriff's department of the valuable crime-deterrent measures your service provides. If your community has a Crime Stop or Neighborhood Watch program, law enforcement personnel may spread the word about your services. And, heaven forbid, should you arrive to find a client's home has been burglarized and call law enforcement officials, they will be familiar with your business. The following is a sample of the letter I used to inform law enforcement officials about my new business:

Law Enforcement Introduction Letter

XYZ Pet Sitters, Inc.
123 Any Where Street
Anytown, USA 20002

Dear Chief _____:

Enclosed you will find information describing XYZ Pet Sitters, Inc. Our service involves going into customers' homes to care for their pets while they are away on vacation or business. We feel that an important part of our service is giving the home a lived-in look by bringing in mail and newspapers, opening and closing curtains and alternating lights—all measures that we hope will be crime deterrents. Although we certainly hope we never encounter a home that has been burglarized, in the event that we do, our staff has been instructed to leave the premises immediately and contact appropriate law enforcement officials.

As spring and summer approach, we anticipate being very busy in the city and county area. For this reason we wanted to make you and your department aware of our service and our sincere desire to have a good working relationship with the police department. If our brochures can be incorporated into any of the community-watch or crime-stoppers programs, we will be happy to supply literature or assist in any way we can. Each of our pet sitters is bonded, insured, reliable, responsible and hard working.

We appreciate the fine efforts of your department and thank you for notifying your staff that our service is available.

Should you or your departmental members have any further questions regarding XYZ Pet Sitters, Inc., please give us a call.

Sincerely yours,

XYZ Pet Sitters, Inc.

- *Friends and family members.* Get your brochures to those who know you and will support you in your new venture. Everybody knows or works with someone who has a pet and that someone just may be interested in using your services. A personal recommendation also means a lot in this business, so get your friends and family members to spread the word about your unique service.

- *Local businesses and companies.* Obtain a list from your local Chamber of Commerce of the major employers in your area. Then send your brochure to the personnel departments of these companies. Often benefits managers in these departments are on the lookout for services and information that will be useful to their employees. They may print a blurb about your service in their company newsletter or post your brochure on employee bulletin boards or in the company cafeteria. Consider offering an introductory discount to their employees for a limited time to make their communication efforts worthwhile. The following is a copy of the letter I send to corporations:

Company Business Letter

> Dear Employees of Atlas Law Offices:
> Enclosed is our brochure describing how we can be of service to you while you are taking vacations, business trips or working overtime.
> We would appreciate it if you would circulate or post our brochure on an employee bulletin board or mention us in your company newsletter. Please call if you need more information or additional brochures.
> Thank you for your time and consideration.
> Sincerely yours,
>
> XYZ Pet Sitters, Inc.

- *Civic clubs and nonprofit organizations.* Obtain a list of these from your local Chamber of Commerce and, again, send your brochure and introductory letter to each. By offering their members an introductory discount, you may entice them to announce your letter and circulate your brochure at their next group meeting.

Also, if you're comfortable with public speaking, offer to give a talk about your new business at their club's next scheduled meeting. Guest speakers are often in demand and you'll find most audiences interested in your talk and appreciative of your visit. Plus, after meeting you personally, some group members will feel confident about giving your service a try. If just the thought of public speaking gets your knees shaking, remember that most people share this fear to some degree. The fact that you're willing to get up and talk about your business will be admired and after a few speeches, you'll be a lot more at ease with making public presentations. The following is a sample of an introductory letter:

Civic Clubs and Nonprofit Organizations

> Dear Arts Council Members:
> Enclosed you will find our brochure, which describes the services of XYZ Pet Sitters, Inc. We have been caring for pets in the area since 1983. We are trying to reach all pet owners in the community before the summer vacation season begins. We would appreciate so much your circulation of our brochure at your next meeting. Any member of your organization using our service before _____ will receive a 10-percent discount on our services. (He or she must identify him or herself as a member of your organization.)
> Please call if you need more brochures or if we can provide additional information.
> Sincerely yours,
>
> XYZ Pet Sitters, Inc.

- *Apartment complexes.* Using the Yellow Pages, call all apartment complexes in your service area to determine which allow pets. Then, send your brochure to the apartment managers of these complexes and ask that they inform resident pet owners of your services. Many apartment complexes provide a "welcome packet" of information to new residents, and your brochure may be added. Inquire about this possibility. The following is a copy of the letter I mailed to apartment complex managers:

Apartment Complex Letter

Dear Manager of Cross Creek Apartments:

Enclosed is our brochure describing the services of XYZ Pet Sitters, Inc. We have been caring for pets in the area since 1983. Because your apartment complex allows pets, we would appreciate your posting our brochure in a conspicuous location. Please let me know if you would be interested in incorporating our brochure into your apartment's welcome material for new residents. I will be happy to provide you with additional brochures.

Thank you for spreading the word about our services. We look forward to caring for the pets at your apartment complex.

Sincerely yours,

XYZ Pet Sitters, Inc.

- *Condominium complexes.* Condominiums are springing up everywhere. My experience has shown they appeal to young professionals who may travel a lot in their occupations and be in need of your services. Most condominiums have a governing board made up of residents. Get your brochures to these board members for display in their clubhouse or inclusion in their resident newsletter.

  Note: Do not go out and stuff brochures in mailboxes or doorways. Stuffing mailboxes (without postage and mail service) is a crime, and most apartments and condominiums adhere to a strict "no solicitation" policy. You can create a negative image of your business by engaging in these tactics.

- *Bulletin boards.* You may not have noticed these before, but they are showing up in more and more places. Grocery stores, restaurants, laundromats and recreation facilities often have one available for the public's use. Start looking (and encourage your sitters to do so) and taking advantage of these to post your business card, brochure or flyer. It's a great form of free advertising!

- *Local colleges and schools.* These institutions have employees and students (and bulletin boards) who are likely to be pet owners. Send your brochure to the language, anthropology, archeology and geography departments (to name a few) at these schools. Professors often organize field trips, and someone in their group may be glad to hear of your services.

Ad Sample

```
┌─────────────────────────────────────────┐
│                                         │
│       XYZ PET SITTERS, INC.             │
│           123 Any Street                │
│       Anywhere, U. S. A. 20002          │
│           (909)  999-8877               │
│                                         │
│        You Can Trust Your Pet to Us     │
│    ● FEED, WATER AND EXERCISE YOUR PETS IN │
│      THE COMFORT OF YOUR HOME           │
│    ● INDIVIDUAL LOVING ATTENTION        │
│    ● MAKE YOUR HOME LOOK "LIVED IN"      │
│                                         │
│  INSURED   999-8877   BONDED            │
└─────────────────────────────────────────┘
```

- *Get involved.* Whether it's the YMCA, United Way, your local Humane Society or another charity, get involved. Represent your company by volunteer participation in your community. Not only will you benefit personally, you will also get the word out about your business to those with whom you serve.

- *Business meetings, seminars, lectures.* Seek out resources that are available in your community for the business owner. There are often lectures and workshops sponsored by the Chamber of Commerce, Small Business Administration, Internal Revenue Service or by professional groups that will help you in various aspects of running your business. These are sometimes free or offered at a nominal charge. They provide a learning experience and are valuable "networking" sessions. You meet others in the business world and at the same time get the opportunity to advertise your pet-sitting service.

- *Church activities.* Don't forget that church socials, committee meetings and circle groups consist of people who'll welcome the news of your pet-sitting services. Inform your congregation about your new business and ask for their support.

- *News releases.* These can be worth their weight in gold with the free publicity they may generate for you. Write an informative news release about the opening of your pet-sitting service and mail it to local television programs, radio stations and newspapers. Follow up these mailings with a phone call to determine if any of the media is interested in interviewing you about your new service from either a human interest or business angle. If they "bite" and put you on the local evening news, this is valuable "free" advertising most small business owners could rarely afford to pay for! Aggressively go after it. The section "Newspapers," shows a sample of a news release.

- *Discounts.* As mentioned earlier, offering discounts to employee groups or customers referred to you by dog groomers, travel agents and so on, can be a terrific form of advertising. It's especially helpful in encouraging new customers to give your service a try. Discounts can also boost business during slow periods or help in getting your business off the ground. Once customers have used you and have been pleased with your services, you know they'll become repeat customers.

GOING TO THE MARDI GRAS?

XYZ PET SITTERS, INC.

Announces 10% off

- FEED, WATER AND EXERCISE YOUR PETS IN THE COMFORT OF YOUR HOME.
- We're Bonded and Insured

123 Any Street
Anywhere, U. S. A. 20002
(909) 999-8877

"You Can Trust Your Pet to Us"

- *Prepare a visual presentation.* Put together a slide show or short video presentation showing your services in action. Offer to show this program at Board of Realtor meetings, garden club meetings, travel fairs and other community events and meetings. Again, if you're inexperienced or uncomfortable with public speaking, now may be the time for you to put your fears aside or to overcome them for the sake of your business.

- *Pleased customers.* The best form of advertising your business can have is the client who praises your services. Sometimes a service business can be slower in growing because it often depends on word-of-mouth recommendations to increase clientele and sales. Although word-of-mouth advertising may take longer to produce growth for your business, it's still the greatest advertising around. To motivate clients to tell others about your business, try offering a discount or gift certificate on future services for each referral they send you. At the very least, send a thank you note for their recommendation of your service.

- *Open your eyes.* Watch not only for bulletin boards but also for pets in cars with their owners. Keep your business cards and brochures with you at all times—you never know when you may need one. If I see a pet waiting in a car for its owner, I slip a brochure under the car's windshield wiper. If I see a pet owner out walking a dog, I stop and ask if they've heard of our pet-sitting service. Yes, some assertiveness is necessary to run a successful business. Take advantage of all "free opportunities" to inform the public about your pet-sitting business and suggest that your staff members do the same. One of my ingenious pet sitters has even started studying the shopping carts in line with her at the grocery store. If she spots pet food in the cart, she strikes up a conversation with the person in line and tells them about our services.

- *Look for promotion and new hire announcements.* These appear in your local newspaper or business publications and newsletters. Send these folks one of your brochures and business cards, along with a personal note either congratulating their achievement or welcoming them to your community. End your note by saying you hope they'll call if you can be of service to them during business or pleasure travel.

- *Seize all free opportunities.* And don't forget opportunities arising at cocktail parties, PTA meetings, diet groups, exercise classes, Christmas parades, craft shows, bowling leagues, day care centers—whatever you (and your sitters) do when you're not actually working in your pet-sitting business. I am always stressing to new pet sitters the importance of taking advantage of all opportunities to educate others about our valuable services, and I love the following advertising stories shared with me by some ingenious pet sitters.

A pet-sitting couple was engaged to care for a dog whose owners said their dog loved to listen to classical music. The owners requested that the radio be left on a classical music station during their absence for the dog's enjoyment. The ingenious pet sitters wrote to the radio station, informing them of their four-legged fan. Loving the story, the radio station called the pet sitters and ended up doing an hour-long interview with them about their pet-sitting service that was interspersed with music having an animal-related title! Needless to say, this was invaluable advertising that resulted in several new clients for the astute pet sitters!

Another advertising technique I love is from the pet sitter whose wife is a dental hygienist. Her dental room is filled with pictures

of their animals, which usually elicits comments or questions from the patient as cleaning preparations take place. This gives her the perfect opportunity to subtly bring up the fact that her husband is a pet sitter . . . and then she launches into telling the patient about her husband's business while cleaning their teeth. The patient is a captive audience who often was unaware that such a service was available in the community. Voila! A new customer for her husband!

One last advertising technique that is very innovative involves utilizing the free public service announcements provided by radio and television stations during inclement weather periods. Many stations run a list or make announcements of the businesses that will either be open or closed for business. Some pet-sitting firms take advantage of this to announce that their service *will* be open—because pet sitters, like postal carriers, usually make rounds during rain, sleet, snow or sun! This public announcement advertises the sitting firm's name as well as assures and impresses the public that pets are cared for during periods of bad weather!

As these ideas illustrate, there are numerous ways to make the public aware of your pet-sitting service. So, now that I've convinced you of the advertising value found in a brochure, business card, business letterhead and postage stamp, let's move on to other advertising techniques.

INEXPENSIVE WAYS TO ADVERTISE

- *Plastic badges.* Invest a few dollars in a plastic lapel badge that has your business name, logo and your name printed on it. *Wear it all the time!* People read these, and you'll be amazed at the number of times people will inquire about your occupation. Store clerks, waiters and waitresses, post office personnel—these are just a few who asked about my pet-sitting service simply from reading my badge.

  Note: Wear your badge when going to a customer's home for an initial interview. It lets the customer know who's at the door and presents an official and professional image for a sitter.

- *Magnetic car plates.* These are a bit more expensive than plastic lapel badges, but well worth their cost in the advertising they generate for your business. My car signs received so much attention and brought in so many new customers, I wish I had invested in them when first opening my business. I highly recommend you give this purchase top priority in your advertising budget. And, if you drive a truck or all-terrain vehicle, consider having a magnetic strip made for the back. Drivers behind you at stoplights will then be jotting your phone number down! Shop around for the best price on magnetic signs.

  Note: When you're driving around town with your business signs for all the world to see, make sure you drive in a careful manner. As noted earlier, you don't want people associating XYZ Pet Sitters with speed demons.

  Also, when making pet-sitting rounds, take the magnetic plates off your doors. Otherwise, your clients and their homes will not remain confidential, as you have assured them they will be. The signs are easy to remove and replace on your car doors.

- *Personalized license plates.* These have become very popular in recent years and just like the magnetic car signs, they provide a terrific form of relatively inexpensive advertising. Although some

pet sitters do not like the vanity license plates because they're afraid the license plate will advertise that the homes they are parked outside are unoccupied, I thought the exposure they provided to drivers behind me at stoplights was more beneficial than the likelihood of causing a burglary at someone's home. And, I was often approached for a business card by someone who read my license plate in the parking lot of a supermarket or shopping center. You'll have to determine if this is a good advertising idea in your area.

- *Costumes.* Rent (or make) a cute animal costume and then walk city streets during lunch hours, handing out your brochures! A cute costumed "animal" (you or someone you've hired) may show up at all kinds of places. Of course, you'll need to get permission for a costumed pet to appear, but investigate the possibilities of outdoor concerts, children's story hours at the library (parents go too), craft fairs, street festivals and dog and cat shows. It's a relatively inexpensive and well-received means of advertising.

- *T-shirts or sweatshirts.* With the popularity of T-shirts and sweatshirts these days, a well-designed shirt will advertise your business for you! I had numerous people stop me to inquire about our services after reading my shirt! Plus, they make a great pet-sitting "uniform" that can easily be laundered. Your customers may be interested in your shirts, too, so company T-shirts could be profitable. Shop around before placing an order; prices do vary. If you don't want to invest in personalized clothing initially, consider purchasing promotional pet-sitting clothing such as that sold by Pet Sitters International. See the Addenda for ordering information.

- *City or County tax office.* Most counties require dog owners to list dogs and pay the appropriate tax assessed on these pets. Dog tags are issued to pet owners from this annual tax listing. You may be able to purchase (or copy) names and addresses of dog owners from your tax office's master list. You could then mail these pet owners information about your pet-sitting service. Time and money will be required to do a mass mailing of this sort, but it's a great way of directly reaching people who may need your services. Taking this idea a step further, you can include a pre-sitting questionnaire with your mailing. This could be a postcard-size form that dog owners could quickly fill out and mail back, indicating preliminary interest in your services. The business this mailing may generate could far exceed the costs involved.

- *Programs and bulletins.* Explore the many activities in your community that use printed programs with advertising space. Some of these include: Little Theater programs, high school sports programs, symphony sponsors, professional/minor league sports promotions, Junior League newsletters, ski or diving club bulletins and a host of others. Advertising on this smaller scale is generally cheaper than other media and gives you a known target group. You can also use these advertisements to offer introductory discounts to ski club members or, for example, to symphony season ticket holders.

- *Posters.* Posters can also be helpful in getting the word out about your business. Because they are generally larger than the business flyer or brochure, they are more easily noticed on community bulletin boards. You may want to check into the cost of having some of these printed for your business.

  > *Tip:* Include tear-off phone number strips along the bottom of your promotional posters. This gives you a way to see if the advertising is working for you, and it's convenient for viewers who are interested in services but may not have a pen available to take down your phone number. I know of some pet sitters who have their posters printed in a pad form. which allows interested pet owners to simply tear off a flyer.

- *Specialty items.* These include magnets, pens, pet food lids, keychains and pet-theme calendars, to name a few that can be imprinted with the name of your business. Although such items are a good form of advertising, they become expensive when given out to the general public. My experience has shown that most pet sitters use the specialty items as a way to say "thank you" to their clients. They mail a calendar with an annual holiday card, or they leave a refrigerator magnet during the last visit of a sitting assignment. Such items also make nice giveaways at pet fairs or business expositions. If you look into specialty items for your business, it's a good idea to shop around for the best price.

- *Gift certificates.* You're sure to be approached for donations to area fund-raisers by civic groups, churches and so on. Consider donating a gift certificate for a weekend of free pet sitting or for a dollar amount that can be redeemed by the recipient. You usually receive free advertising in exchange for the donation and I found the contribution usually resulted in the recipient becoming a repeat customer. This repeat business more than paid for the donated services—plus, the donation was a legitimate business expense.

However, give some thought to your policy on such contributions. There are a lot of fund-raising organizations that will be asking for your support!

- *Adopt-A-Highway.* Many states have implemented this kind of program to help keep roads and highways "clean and green." Area businesses adopt a certain section of a road or highway and agree to clean the sides of it of litter on a regular basis. In exchange, the state will erect a road sign that states the name of the business responsible for that portion of road or highway. This is valuable advertising as well as a good program to become involved in. Contact your state department of transportation to see if this program exists.

- *"Lead groups."* These groups, also known as networks, are a new marketing phenomenon in many cities. A "lead group" consists of a variety of business people or entrepreneurs who meet weekly or monthly for a breakfast, lunch or social hour. The purpose behind the group is to help build each other's businesses by sharing business leads. Usually a lead club allows only one member from an occupation to belong, for example, one insurance agent, exterminator, printing company, plumber, banker and so on. The club members utilize the businesses and services of their Lead Club members when applicable, as well as refer friends, family and coworkers. It's a great way to meet area professionals and advertise your pet-sitting services. The membership costs are usually nominal and most cities have several such clubs from which to choose. If a pet-sitting firm already belongs to the first club you contact, try another one—or start a new lead group! Check the business section of your newspaper or Yellow Pages for these networking groups.

Very early on I learned that pet owners come in all shapes and sizes—from different economic levels and with a wide range of interests. So, it's difficult—and unwise—to pinpoint one specific group for advertising purposes. The one thing pet owners do have in common is a genuine love of their pets. Keep this in mind and try to reach all types of pet owners in your advertising efforts.

REACHING THE MASSES—THAT IS THE QUESTION

The best way to reach a large number of people with your advertising message is through newspaper, radio, television and Yellow Pages. However, these are usually the most expensive forms of advertising and, unless your goal is to operate a larger-scale pet-sitting service, there's really no reason to reach the masses. To do so would only waste your revenues and time as you answer phone calls only to tell callers that you don't service their neighborhood area, or that you're not taking new clients now. If your plan is to pet sit on a small scale, the less expensive advertising ideas should work well for you. Some of these ideas, along with word of mouth, will soon build your clientele to the point you want. You can skip the rest of this section if you so desire!

However, if you're planning to utilize a staff of pet sitters and want to cover a large route with sitting services, these advertising options will help you to build your business much faster. My experiences and opinions about these four advertising techniques follow.

NEWSPAPERS

Advertising in the newspaper will get you results. But before you take out an expensive display ad, try this suggestion first. Send out a news release (discussed in detail earlier in this chapter). Using news releases is such a good idea that it's worth repeating. Deliver or mail your news release to the business editor of your local newspaper(s). The openings of new businesses are often considered newsworthy enough to rate a free paragraph on the business page. Some smaller or rural newspapers will even run a full-fledged article free, announcing the opening and details of your business. And, because pet sitting is a relatively new concept in some areas, your business will intrigue newspaper reporters. From a human interest standpoint, pet sitting has potential for a good story. Your service can be approached from the angle of its uniqueness, its potential to deter crime, or its female-ownership (if applicable). Call reporters assigned to human interest articles, as well as radio and television stations, to inquire if anyone would like to interview you for a story. If so, you're on your way.

Often these stories do more to promote your business and lend credibility than any amount of paid advertising. For more information on news releases, please see Chapter 6, "Public Relations," section titled "News Releases."

News Release

Date: May 1, 1997   For further information contact:
For: XYZ Pet Sitters, Inc.   Jane Smith, President
For Release: Immediately

New Pet-Sitting Business Opens in Piedmont

Winston-Salem, N. C. . . . Area pet owners now have an alternate choice for pet care during vacation and business trips. Jane Smith, president, has opened XYZ Pet Sitters, Inc., at 1234 Anywhere Street. The unique service provided by the company means that pet owners can now leave their household pet(s) in the comfort and familiarity of home.

"One of our insured and bonded staff members will visit a home on a daily basis to feed, water and care for the pet(s). And, most importantly, we'll provide lots of tender loving care and personalized attention during each visit," says Smith, president of the newly formed company.

XYZ Pet Sitters, Inc., has a staff of eight professional pet sitters, all of whom truly love pets and have been thoroughly trained by the company. Not only do they all look after household pets in pampered style, they also are happy to bring in newspapers, mail and even water houseplants. "We want every pet owner to be able to leave home with peace of mind, knowing his or her pet(s) and home are in our responsible care," notes Smith.

All clients making reservations for pet-sitting services during the month of May will receive a 10-percent discount off the total sitting fee. "This offer is to introduce our services to Piedmont pet owners and is part of our grand opening celebration," says Smith. To get additional information or to make a reservation, call XYZ Pet Sitters, Inc., at 999-8811.

Note: When possible, it's a good idea to check stories and articles before publication or broadcast. You want to ensure that your comments were not misconstrued, and that the story presents you and your business favorably.

In addition to any free media coverage you may receive, you will need to buy some advertising. An inexpensive form of newspaper advertising is to run a short classified ad about your service under the "Pets" heading. The following are sample classified ads:

Sample Classified Ads

Looking for a pet sitter? Ask your vet about us. XYZ Pet Sitters. 999-8877. Bonded and insured.

Need a pet sitter? See our display ad on page 345 of the Yellow Pages. XYZ Pet Sitters. 999-8877.

These classified ads are great because they say a lot in only a few words. However, before running similar copy, make sure you can count on a good reference from area veterinarians, that you are bonded and insured and that you are running an ad in the Yellow Pages!

Some newspapers have a "Consumer Review" or "Business Review" section which, for a fee, will run an article and picture about your business. These are sometimes called advertorials. Check to see if your newspaper publishes neighborhood inserts or a special pet page section. If so, ads in these sections are usually less expensive because the inserts only reach readers in certain zip codes. I advertised in each of these sections many times and always received an excellent response.

The most successful newspaper advertising campaign I ran for my business became what is now called, "PZZZ...Ads." These were a series of ads depicting photos of a pet in holiday or seasonal attire with a short phrase imparting a message about my services. The photos were eye-catching and humorous—and increased my business tremendously. The ad series was very popular—with pet owners and non–pet owners as well! I had one lady tell me she didn't have any pets but she loved my cute ads so much she clipped them each week and posted them on her office bulletin board for coworkers to see. The "PZZZ...Ads" are now available for purchase (see the Addenda for ordering information). If you prefer to design your own display ads, a small one with a catchy phrase underneath, such as "Holiday Travel?" or "Business Travel?" or "Going on Vacation?" will also get noticed.

When the American Animal Hospital Association (AAHA) asked who cares for the family cat or dog, their findings showed that in 66 percent of American families, it's mom. I found this to be true in the ten years I operated my pet-sitting business—seven out of ten calls for services were usually made by the female in the household! Keep this in mind when targeting your newspaper advertising. If your newspaper has a daily or weekly women's section or food section, these could provide good placement for your ad. Advertising in the travel, entertainment, sports and business sections can also be effective.

I found advertising in Sunday through Wednesday papers to bring a better response than Thursday through Saturday, because those are the days people tend to travel and, therefore, miss the daily local newspaper. Because display advertising tends to be expensive, I primarily advertised before holidays, during the summer vacation months, and on the anniversary date of my business opening. (Announcing the birthday or age of your business lends further credibility—it shows you have staying power and are not a fly-by-night operation.)

Newspaper advertising does get noticed and creates name recognition with repetition. If the ad is distinctive, people will remember it long after the newspaper has been discarded.

Note: If you operate your pet-sitting service in an extremely large city, newspaper advertising may not be the wisest use of your advertising dollar. First, the cost may be prohibitive. Second, it may result in an annoying number of crank calls. Third, you may not even cover the entire city with pet-sitting services. So, give careful thought before using any form of mass media advertising. And, when you do, be sure to specify the areas you serve to make maximum use of your advertising dollar.

When possible, plan your newspaper advertising months in advance to take advantage of contract rates. Ask the advertising sales representative you work with about available contract rates.

YELLOW PAGES

Advertising in the Yellow Pages of your local telephone directory is another way of reaching a mass audience. Although it is expensive for the small business, it's a necessary expenditure—especially when you're just getting started. This is because people who need a service often consult the Yellow Pages for providers. And, because pet sitting is still a new service in some areas, there are some pet owners who may not be aware that in-home care is even an option. When making travel plans, they are likely to consult the Yellow Pages for boarding kennels, but not for pet sitters. This is why you need an eye-catching ad that describes your alternative service.

In the past, pet sitters had little choice about the placement of Yellow Page ads. We were automatically lumped under the heading of "Kennels" or "Dog and Cat Boarding/Exercising," although neither accurately reflects the care we provide. This has not been all bad though. After all, with pet sitting still a new concept, many pet owners aren't aware of our personalized services and don't know to look for us, unless they see our listing with the more traditional boarding or kennel option. With pet sitting growing and gaining in popularity, more telephone books offer the option of listing under "Pet Sitters" or "Sitting Services." It's a good idea to have a dual listing under "Pet Sitters" and "Kennels," if both are available to you.

In the first year or two of your business, you need an enticing display ad, or at least something larger than the normal, free phone listing a business receives. You want to let the world know your service is available. After you've established a reputation, just your business name, number and perhaps a descriptive slogan in the Yellow Pages will suffice.

My initial experience with advertising in the Yellow Pages was not especially positive (perhaps clouded by an overly aggressive salesperson). But the results of advertising surveys—of my own pet-sitting clients and of other pet-sitting firms—have shown that Yellow Page ads are consistently among the top five methods of bringing in new customers. Usually it's a year-long advertising contract with the Yellow Pages that can seem like a tremendous expense to the small business owner—but just consider it a necessary evil of being in a service business!

TELEVISION

Some time ago I attended a workshop for small businesses. A local advertising executive spoke. After his presentation, I told him about my pet-sitting service and asked where I should put my advertising dollar. His emphatic reply was "television." I gasped, thinking big money, but he pointed out that families have pets, and families stay at home and watch television. Families also take vacations. He pointed out that retired people and housewives watch daytime television, and working people watch morning news programs and night programming. In short, everyone watches television. According to him, the phenomenal number of people you can reach through television advertising makes it a bargain for your advertising dollar. So, with his advice in mind, I pursued advertising on a local TV station.

I quickly discovered that television advertising, indeed, is not cheap, but it is a lot more affordable than I had imagined. The station sales representative worked with me to tailor a commercial that would convey my message to the targeted viewing audience. Filming and starring in the commercial was an interesting and fun experience. I was both thrilled and proud when I saw the finished product for the first time in the studio. And when I saw my commercial on television, I felt my business had arrived.

Nevertheless, it was difficult to assess the effect of the television ads. Was the large expenditure worth the return? And what exactly was the return on my investment? It was hard for me to measure the effectiveness of radio and television commercials because of the nature of our product. In-home pet care is not something like food or cleaning products that are needed or used daily. A pet owner may see or listen to your commercial at Thanksgiving, but not need your services until the first week of July, though it was because of your radio or television ad that he or she learned of your service.

The television advertising I did was with a local affiliate of one of the major networks. Now that cable stations have multiplied the number of options from which to choose, television advertising has become more affordable. Plus, in many cases, there are advertising packages available that allow you so many commercials on three or four cable networks of your choice. Talk with a cable advertising representative to see what advertising packages are available. He or she may suggest that in order to reach business travelers you might elect to run your pet-sitting commercial on CNN, ESPN, The Discovery Channel and The History Channel. Homemakers may be tuned into Lifetime, Arts & Entertainment, American Movie Classics and so on. Cable television commercials may be the more affordable and selective way to go for today's pet sitter.

RADIO

I have mixed feelings about this form of advertising. Calls for our services did come in the days my radio commercials were broadcast. However, I'm not convinced that the business generated from the commercials paid for the high cost of airing them. Radio advertising is expensive for the small business owner; I recommend that you reserve its use until after you've gotten your business off the ground and have some advertising dollars to spare.

Should you decide to pursue radio advertising, keep the following in mind. First, do your homework by calling and researching various radio stations. Request Arbitron ratings from each station. *Arbitron* is a company that conducts private surveys to determine which groups listen to what radio station and when they listen. Arbitron periodically publishes these demographic statistics about the listeners for each station. By obtaining this information, you can most effectively determine the right station and time to place your commercial.

When selecting radio stations, choose the ones whose audience profiles your potential customer. Choosing the station you listen to or the one that happens to be the least expensive is not necessarily your best buy. Also, there's no sense in paying a premium price to advertise on a station that covers four counties if you don't provide service to those areas—even if the station is the most popular.

I found that running radio commercials during rush-hour traffic is the most effective time. You reach the working person who takes vacations, may travel on business and who presumably can afford your service.

Monday, Tuesday and Wednesday were the best days to run my radio commercials. As with newspaper ads, the logic is that Thursday through Sunday are more popular vacation days, and your listening audience may not be as large. You want to reach the vacationers before they leave town.

Because talk radio has become so popular in recent years, a better option would be to see what local radio talk shows broadcast in your area. Then, send news releases along with a cover letter offering to be a guest on any business, pet, or community service programs. If you're invited to appear on a talk program, the exposure and credibility it would lend would be far more valuable than any commercial you could pay to run! And, such appearances will help to establish you as an expert in your field. The media will soon begin calling *you* when they need a spokesperson on pets or pet sitting—more free advertising!

During my many years of being involved with professional pet sitting, I conducted several marketing surveys to determine how clients heard about pet sitting. Results of these surveys indicated that the majority of clients learned about us from the following:

1. Word-of-mouth referrals

2. Yellow-Page advertising

3. Newspaper advertising

4. Veterinarian referrals

Among the lowest-rated means of advertising were radio and television. These surveys substantiate that the most expensive forms of advertising definitely were not the most effective for *my* pet-sitting service and quite possibly, they may not be the most effective for *any* pet-sitting service. If I had it to do over again, I would have put more money, sooner, into Yellow-Page and newspaper advertising—it definitely would have helped my business grow faster.

The best advice I can give to today's new pet sitter is to concentrate your efforts on doing a terrific job for your clients, so they will enthusiastically tell others about your services. After all, a word-of-mouth referral is generally considered to be the best means of advertising for any business.

THE FAMILIAR IMAGE

In whatever advertising you do, continuity is important. Think of advertising campaigns for products or services you see every day. Surely the name of a local real estate company comes to your mind just from a glimpse of the design and colors of its for-sale signs posted throughout your community. You probably don't even need to read the signs. Remember, continuity and repeated exposure are crucial. Put some thought, time and dollars into a logo, slogan, company color(s), brochure and ad design to promote your business; then get them out and keep them out for the public to see. You want your image to be so professional and your name so familiar that the public begins to think there's something wrong in not having a "personal pet sitter" from your organization.

> *Note:* Another bit of advice from my years of experience is that animals get noticed. If you want the public to notice, include animals in your advertising—whether it's a photograph, poster or television commercial.

MORE GREAT ADVERTISING IDEAS FROM READERS

At the back of this book you'll see where I ask readers to write to me and share things that help their pet-sitting businesses to be successful. The pet-sitting industry is very fortunate to have such caring and dedicated members who do take the time to write and share ideas, tips and suggestions. Here are some advertising ideas offered by previous readers of this book.

- Advertise on hospital bulletin boards because people with broken legs or recent surgeries can't walk their dogs!
- Always carry business cards with you when walking a dog—conversations always strike up with other owners out walking and business cards come in handy!
- Be sure to place business cards and brochures at area feed stores.

The following are great sources from which to rent mailing lists for direct mail campaigns: alumni groups, PTA memberships, church memberships, country club memberships and attendees of private schools.

Advertising ideas that worked well for some pet sitters and not at all for others, according to my mail, include the following:

- Ads on plastic phone book covers
- Val-Pak (direct mail) coupons
- Movie theater advertisements
- Ads on the back of grocery store receipts

    Note: Many thanks to the readers who submitted these ideas. Although I can't personally credit each submission, you know who you are! Your suggestions are appreciated and help to make the road to success much easier for new pet sitters!

CHAPTER 6

PUBLIC RELATIONS

If running your own business is new to you, you may not be aware of what public relations is and how important it can be to your business. There is a difference between advertising and public relations, although it can sometimes seem like a fine line between the two. Both result in exposure and public image. Advertising is normally considered to be a paid announcement; the promotion that comes from public relations is typically free media exposure.

Webster's New World Dictionary defines public relations as "relations with the general public as through publicity; specifically those functions of a corporation, organization, etc. concerned with attempting to create favorable public opinion for itself." Public relations can be a very credible—and inexpensive—method of communicating to the public the benefits and features of in-home pet-care services. As a professional pet sitter, there are many community activities you can become involved with that will demonstrate your civic spirit and increase your personal visibility. This visibility means business that can directly affect your company's bottom line.

Whether you choose to volunteer at your local Humane Society, serve on a church committee, or sponsor a Little League team, you accomplish several things:

- You show your concern for the town or city in which you live. Those who participate with you may decide to do business with you because of your involvement.

- You'll derive personal satisfaction from your goodwill efforts.
- Some form of publicity that benefits you professionally often results from the involvement.

The publicity that comes from public relations endeavors is often more valuable than what the small business owner could ever afford to buy in the way of advertising. The good public image that it creates can attract attention for your business and give you an edge over your competition. Exposure from public relations activities helps establish you as an authority and leader in your field; in addition, it helps create a desire for your pet-sitting services and adds to the public's confidence in them.

Besides involvement with animal-related programs such as pet therapy visits to nursing homes or hospitals or business-related activities, such as serving on the membership committee of your local Chamber of Commerce, there are several other public relations options that may be of interest to you. Some of these are discussed in this chapter.

DEVELOPING A NEWSLETTER

Consider producing a monthly, quarterly or semiannual newsletter for your business. Sending out a company newsletter provides an effective means of advertising and it's a great public relations tool. A newsletter allows you to communicate with your clients and provide them with useful information, thereby lending credibility and sincerity to your business endeavors.

In the company newsletters I produced, I always followed the same format. This practice saved time and money because I didn't have to create each newsletter anew. A familiar format also increased recognition among my customers—they didn't mistake my newsletter for junk mail!

As the business owner, I wrote a personal column to inform clients of any changes in our business or payment procedures. I also used this column to thank customers for using our services.

Each newsletter contained informative material on pet care, pet products or pet-related organizations. Pet sitters have the opportunity to influence customers in healthful practices for their pets and to educate them about the latest in products, foods, toys and so on. Your newsletter can provide a wonderful way to educate your clients—but of course, first you must educate yourself before sharing any such information. Another idea is to invite local veterinarians to provide short articles on topics of interest to pet owners. Many veterinarians will do this free of charge or for a small fee because of their commitment to the welfare of animals.

Other typical columns I usually included in my newsletters were:

- *Sitter profiles.* A brief introduction about a couple of pet sitters; their sitting routes, hobbies or special interests and the type of pets they own or specialize in.

- *Seasonal tips.* Hot- or cold-weather concerns for pets, holiday hazards and so on.

- *Customer profile.* This would appear if a client took an exotic trip or had an interesting job or hobby—clients love the notoriety of being profiled!

- *Interesting vacation destinations.* A local travel agent provided this column in exchange for an ad in the newsletter.

- *Pet-sitting stories and anecdotes.* Share an experience that has happened to you or a staff pet sitter. Humorous stories and anecdotes are entertaining, while serious stories often contain a "lesson" or send a message to the reader.

- *Pet-related cartoon or joke.* If you aren't artistic, hire a graphic-arts student or freelancer to do a cartoon. Please don't use any cartoons from newspapers or magazines without receiving written permission from the cartoonist or publisher. And, make sure any jokes or cartoons you include are not possibly offensive to your readers.

- *Industry news.* Announcement of the PSI "Pet Sitter of the Year" contest, National Professional Pet Sitters Week observances and so on.

It's best to stay away from controversial subjects that may offend some customers in your newsletter. Although it can be tempting to use it as a sounding board, it's wise to keep it light, interesting and entertaining.

Your newsletter provides a service of useful information to your clients, but you can and should use it to generate business as well. Take advantage of it to announce special promotions, to publish discount coupons or even to place help-wanted ads. (Some of your customers may be interested in pet sitting or know someone who is looking for part-time work.)

Printing a newsletter is relatively inexpensive. If you have a computer, there are many publishing software programs available now that will make easy work of designing a newsletter. But even having it done by a print shop is affordable, especially if you shop around. The largest expense will be your postage for mailing the newsletter. If you plan a frequent mailing schedule, you should consider obtaining a bulk-mail permit from your post office. The permit will greatly decrease your postage costs with mass mailings. Or, explore the possibility of having a mailing house handle your bulk mailings. They usually have a bulk permit available for use by customers.

Many pet sitters offset the costs of producing a company newsletter by selling advertising space. By offering even a few business-card-size ads, you'll help the newsletter pay for itself. With a few more ads, your newsletter could become profitable! Veterinarians, groomers, pet stores, travel agents, house-cleaning and lawn-care services, home security systems and your clients who have a product or service may be interested in advertising to your clientele.

Your newsletter (crossing that fine line between public relations and advertising!) can be a great advertisement for your business. Keep a supply on hand and mail one out with your brochure to potential clients who request information about your services. They also can be left in the waiting rooms of veterinarian, doctor and dentist offices (make sure you obtain permission to leave them). Advertisers (groomers, pet stores and so on) also are likely to let you display newsletters in their places of business.

Publishing a newsletter can be one of the best things you do for your pet-sitting business. My clients indicated they genuinely appreciated receiving mine. The pennies per copy it costs to produce go a long way in showing our customers we appreciate them and are serious about pet sitting as a profession.

Note: If you use any previously published material in your newsletter, make sure you obtain permission to do so. Plagiarism and copyright infringement are serious infractions of the law.

From the mailbag: A reader wrote to tell me she had implemented a "Favorite Customer Comments" column in her newsletter. This is where she reprinted compliments taken from evaluation forms or excerpts from notes attached to payments. This practice showed the clientele how much their praise was appreciated—and probably encouraged some clients to consider offering it! Great idea!

NEWS RELEASES

News releases, or press releases as they are sometimes called, are exactly what the name implies—they release news to the media. And, when the media uses your release—in a newspaper or magazine or on a radio or television broadcast—you receive invaluable publicity. News releases can be worth their weight in gold. You'll be smart to utilize them in your business as often as possible.

News That Is Newsworthy

Chapter 5, "Advertising," discusses the advantages of using news releases in your business under the "Newspapers" section. Here are some instances when you should consider issuing a news release:

- The "grand opening" of your business
- A "new hire" (new pet sitter)
- A promotion
- Any new services you add, such as pet transportation, pet food delivery and so on
- Any awards you or your staff members receive
- Your support of any community needs/projects (such as volunteer activities)
- Membership in business organizations or professional affiliations
- Completion of a pet-sitting accreditation program or educational achievement
- Attendance at a national convention

How to Write a News Release

Guidelines for writing a news release include the following. It may be helpful to review the sample "grand opening" news release on page 148 of this chapter or the one in the "Newspapers" section of Chapter 5 as you read through these pointers.

- Source information (name, address, phone number) appears in upper-right corner.
- The release date appears in the upper-left corner.
- The headline summarizes the content of the release and is typed in capital letters.
- The first paragraph of the release answers who, what, when, where, why and how. Your headline and first paragraph often determine whether the reader (editor) is intrigued enough to read more of your release—or use it!
- Always type a news release; double space and leave wide margins.
- Keep paragraphs and sentences short and to the point.
- Usually the shorter the release, the better. However, if a longer release is needed to do the subject justice, space your pages so one paragraph ends at the bottom of a page and a new paragraph begins at the top of the next page.
- On the last page, the end of the release is indicated by "-O-" or "# # #" or "END." This is normally centered under the final paragraph.
- Carefully proofread for typing or spelling errors.
- Always send a good, clean copy of your news release to the media—preferably on business letterhead.

  Note: A tremendous benefit of membership in an organization like Pet Sitters International is that professionally prepared news releases are made available for use by members with their local media. These are interesting and informative press releases that enhance your credibility on the local level and help increase the success of your business.

Compiling a Media List

Take some time to put together a local media list for your news release mailings. Include newspapers (large and small publications), radio stations, television stations and area magazines. A media list may be available from your Chamber of Commerce. If not, make some phone calls to ascertain the appropriate editor or producer to whose attention the release should be sent. Sometimes the people in these positions change, so make every effort to keep your list current.

After determining the number of news releases you'll need, get them in the mail so that you're consistent with the release date at the top of your news release. If you haven't heard from any editors or producers within a week after mailing, follow up with a phone call. Politely ask if they received the release, if they plan to use it or if they need additional information or a photograph to accompany the article. Don't be discouraged or take it personally if an editor is brief or negative about using your news release. These people receive many news releases and news tips every day. If your first attempts with news releases don't succeed, try again. When your efforts result in free publicity, you'll see that news releases are a worthwhile investment of time and money.

Note: If the story behind your news release can be enhanced by a photograph, it's a good idea to provide one with your mailing. Newspapers have their own photographers, but there are only so many subjects in a day they can cover. Sending a photograph demonstrates the visual impact of your story—even to television news people—that creates interest in generating news coverage. Publicity photos are best when there is action taking place, when the number of people involved is limited and, of course, when an animal is involved! Before taking any photos of clients' pets or homes, be sure to obtain their permission.

Sample News Release

Date: Contact: Amy Smith, 999-8877
For: Business Name   Address (or use business
Release Date: Immediately   letterhead for news release)
NEWS RELEASE   Telephone

UNIQUE PET-SITTING SERVICE TO CELEBRATE GRAND OPENING

Anytown, NC . . . XYZ Pet Sitters, a professional pet-sitting service, will open Monday, April 21. The only business of its type in this area, the new firm will serve pet owners throughout Forsyth county.

---

continues

The unique service will provide in-home pet care as an alternative to kennels or leaving pets in the care of neighbors or friends. The company offers additional services to its clients, such as watering plants, rotating lights, bringing in mail and newspapers and generally giving the home a "lived in" look.

"Our staff will include six pet sitters who have completed a training program and are bonded and insured," says Amy Smith, president of the service agency. "Our goal is to make it much easier for Forsyth county pet owners to travel by using our quality pet-care services." XYZ Pet Sitters is also a member of Pet Sitters International, an educational organization for professional pet sitters.

Interested persons may call 999-8877 for more information or to reserve a pet sitter. XYZ Pet Sitters needs at least four days notice before a client is planning to leave town so a sitter may visit the home, become familiar with the pets, review needed services and confirm the assignment.

# # #

PUBLIC SPEAKING

Yes, I know that speaking in public is one of people's greatest fears because I suffer from it too! According to something I recently read, it is more feared than death or divorce! However, I have found that if you can shake your way through it, public speaking is probably the best free publicity you can get for your business. The good news is that it does get easier the more you do it.

There are numerous opportunities available for guest speakers in most communities. Because people tend to do business with people they know or are at least familiar with, public speaking engagements will greatly increase the likelihood of listeners using your services. Here are some groups you could make a presentation available to:

- *Civic clubs.* Jaycees, Kiwanis, Masons, Elks, Rotarians, and the list goes on and on. See if your Chamber of Commerce has a listing of civic clubs available along with contact information.

- *Business groups.* Chamber of Commerce functions and local professional groups, such as accountants, secretaries, personnel managers, realtors and women's networks hold regular meetings where interesting guest speakers are in demand.

- *Garden clubs.* Even if members do not have pets, they most likely know someone who does or may need their plants watered by your service during absences from home.

- *School children.* A great place to educate about responsible pet care—and the advantages of using a pet sitter! What parent can refuse a child's request to use a pet sitter?!

Keep in mind that few people are born great public speakers—for most of us it takes practice, practice, practice. Write your speech, and practice in front of family, friends and coworkers. This will greatly increase your comfort level. Try to add some humor; everyone enjoys a good laugh, and it will make you, and your audience, more relaxed. Use visual aids when possible (overheads, the public relations video, *What Is Pet Sitting?,* distribution of your brochures and so on) and dress comfortably.

Don't underestimate yourself! Audiences are comprised of people who admire your ability to stand up in front of them and who want to hear what you have to say. You can do this. You don't have to, but believing in your business and the great service you're providing will help to make the task easier. Remember that public speaking will really help your business to grow.

Note: If you should ever hear me at a public speaking engagement, know that the butterflies and nervousness are there, and please be kind!

EXHIBITION BOOTHS

There are many opportunities for booth space rentals in most communities. Although some of these are strictly advertising mediums, such as bridal fairs and travel or business expositions, others are more closely aligned to public relations, such as participating in a pet fair with veterinarians, groomers or animal transport services. Regardless of the event's location, there are some guidelines that may be helpful to maximize the potential from a booth display:

1. Other participants may be much larger companies with prefabricated booth designs. You'll want to make your booth display as professional as possible. Reserve a table from the promoters—these are usually skirted and look nicer.

2. Find out if there is a color theme to the show so you can try to match your display materials to it.

3. If electricity is available, consider having a small television with a VCR at your table. This would allow you to play taped TV spots of your company (if you've appeared on any local programs), pet-sitting videos or pet first-aid/care videos.

4. Use brochure and business card stands to display company literature.

5. Use a fishbowl for a door-prize drawing to be held for free pet-sitting services or a giveaway item. Require names and addresses so you can mail brochures or coupons at a later date.

6. Remember that food attracts people! Have a plate of animal crackers or a dish of candy for visitors. Giveaway items, such as balloons for children or magnets for adults, are also popular. Bookmarks (available from Pet Sitters International) disappear quickly.

7. Purchase some inexpensive frames to showcase collages of customer's pets, association membership documents or your own pets. Old calendars are a good source for eye-catching photographs of pets. Stuffed animals can add visual appeal.

8. Have a nice vinyl or acrylic sign made by a sign company or, if you have a computer and color printer, make some nice banners for your booth.

9 Display your Client Presentation book.

10. Check to see what items are available from Pet Sitters International for use at such shows.

11. If there is a local network of pet sitters in your area, consider jointly renting booth space at exhibitions to increase exposure while holding down costs.

12. Make sure you've arranged for relief help in staffing your booth to allow you time for meals, breaks or to walk around and meet the other exhibitors.

Besides the attending audience you'll reach with exhibition space, most shows receive coverage from local television, radio and newspapers, which can greatly increase your exposure. Forethought and planning will result in a nice booth display you can use again and again. Plus, it will help you to enjoy yourself while promoting your business.

SPECIAL EVENTS

You may prefer to create your own public relations programs. Some ideas for you to consider include:

- *Pet Photo Day.* Hold an event where pet owners can bring their pet(s) for a professional photo (there are many pet photographers out there now and some who travel the country doing fund-raising shoots). Donate the sitting fee to a deserving local animal-related cause.

- *Dog "Ball."* Coordinate a dinner and dance where dogs and their people can both enjoy the festivities. Donate ticket proceeds to an animal-related organization.

- *Dog Walkathon.* Sponsor a morning or afternoon walk at a local park. Give registration fees to an animal-related charity.

- *Halloween Pet Costume Contest.* Sponsor a contest where pet owners can submit photographs of their pets in costume. Charge an entry fee that can be donated to a local pet charity.

- *Profit Sharing.* Donate a percentage of your annual profits to a local pet shelter or charity. Indicate on your company literature that you do this and then issue a news release when you make the annual contribution.

It is the animals who benefit from special fund-raisers like these, but there are benefits for the participating pet sitter as well. Doors will open to you from public relations efforts; however, it is often enough to know you've helped make a difference.

BUSINESS ETIQUETTE

Good business etiquette is an important aspect of public relations. Remember all the people you called upon to help you build your business? The groomers, veterinarians, kennels, travel agents, hairdressers—whomever! It's a good public relations idea to go a step further and thank these folks in some way—after all, you want to stay on their good side!

Saying thanks can involve simply sending a handwritten note on a holiday card or dropping a box of fresh doughnuts off for a morning coffee break. The Christmas season provides a great opportunity to deliver a special gift to those who have contributed to your business's success; however, if you're too busy during this time there's always Valentine's Day or a goodie basket for Easter!

The same etiquette applies to customers as well. If the length of your client list prohibits the sending of holiday cards, then a heartfelt "thanks" in your company newsletter will suffice. For customers who allow you to use them as references or for those who send referrals to you, a gift certificate or coupon for future pet-sitting services will be an appreciated gesture.

Pet sitting, by nature, is a very personal business with the access it provides to people's homes, pets and lives. Practice good business etiquette so you'll enjoy favorable public relations with your business associates.

CHAPTER 7

EXAMINING THE NEGATIVES

Whenever exploring a possible investment or career opportunity, it is important to examine the negatives. I was fortunate in that I experienced very few serious problems, and the positive aspects of running and operating a pet-sitting service have far outweighed the negative ones. I've found that most problems can be solved with a potent combination of common sense and determination; many problems can be avoided or minimized with some forethought and planning.

Since the first edition of this book, many readers have asked me to address the drawbacks of pet sitting. Others have shared problems they've experienced or ones they've anticipated. This chapter is a combination of my experiences and those that readers have shared with me.

The biggest problem is faced mainly by pet sitters who work alone. If you don't have any employees, you may find yourself working nearly 365 days a year. Holidays are especially busy times for pet sitters, so you may find that family celebrations will have to be adjusted around your schedule. Of course, these problems can be remedied or minimized by having a staff of sitters; that way weekend and holiday assignments can be rotated. Or you can choose to operate your service only during certain months of the year, such as May to September. However, there are so many benefits to pet sitting that I've found the sacrifice of working on holidays to be a small concession.

Note: If you plan to work alone, remember that a reputable pet sitter should have provisions made for back-up services. This will allow you and your clients peace of mind should you, for whatever reason, not be able to personally fulfill visits as contracted.

Depending on the area in which you live, weather can occasionally be a drawback to pet sitting. I'll be the first to admit that walking a dog (or several of them!) on a chilly, rainy day can be less than pleasurable, as is sliding around with a dog in six inches of sleet and snow. Still, I can't think of any job that comes without imperfections, can you? When it was a gorgeous spring day and I was out walking those same dogs, well, it was hard to believe I would actually get paid for having so much fun!

A minor drawback to pet sitting is that you can expect to hear an occasional criticism of your fees. When setting your prices, you'll probably find your fees are considerably higher than the local boarding kennel (unless the assignment involves multiple pets—then a pet sitter is usually less expensive than a kennel). Some pet owners are not accustomed to spending so much on their pet whether it's for veterinary care, dietary needs or the TLC you'll be providing. You just have to take this infrequent objection in stride and realize that you provide a specialized service that isn't going to be appreciated or utilized by everyone. Fortunately, many pet owners think the world of their pets and will gladly pay your fees, which are actually reasonable considering the peace of mind your service allows them when they are away from home. My experience was that for every person who complained that my fees were too high, there were probably five who asked, "Is that all you charge?"

Burnout can also be a problem. Although no profession is immune, a pet sitter (especially one who works alone) has to guard against it. Caring for pets can be so enjoyable that you may find yourself having a hard time telling clients "no" or "I'm already booked for next weekend." Not wanting to disappoint a client or lose out on the business, you'll find yourself taking on too much and running yourself ragged. Exhaustion soon leads to burnout. If you rarely have any time off or continually miss out on holiday celebrations, you'll find burnout occurring sooner rather than later. By recognizing that this threat exists, you'll be able to structure your staff accordingly and schedule reservations wisely to prevent burnout from ruining what can be a wonderful career. The best advice I can give you to control your business, rather than letting it (or your customers!) control you, is to learn how to say "no"!

JUST SAY NO

One little word. How can it be so hard to say? Is there something peculiar to the pet-sitting profession that makes saying "no" an impossible feat?

Are we so afraid if we don't accept every last minute reservation or sit for the client with the nasty, filthy home that our business will be doomed for failure? Is it because we're a female-dominated industry or we're just plain ol' nice folks that "no" doesn't seem to belong in our vocabularies? Whatever the cause, it has become obvious that this is an industry-wide problem with which pet sitters must come to terms. Your business success—and sanity—rely heavily on being able to say, simply and confidently, "no."

Eventually, it will happen. You'll be completely booked for the weekend or maybe you even blocked the weekend out for some much-needed time off. About 9:00 P.M. on Friday evening the phone rings with a customer begging you for weekend services. You sigh and accept the job even though it will really stretch you or mean giving up the "time off" you'd planned—and you hate yourself for not saying no!

Or, maybe a customer will complain that your prices are too high and try to get you to lower your fees. You'll hesitate as you think how, on occasion, you feel a little guilty about charges for fun "easy" jobs . . . and this is a beautiful home to visit and maybe you could knock a little off your fee . . . .

Or, perhaps the client will acknowledge on the phone that her dog is territorial and has been known to act aggressively towards strangers. She dismisses these actions with the comment, "if you're a pet-care professional, you won't have any problem." Before you realize it, you've agreed to set up an initial meeting and dread the situation already.

And then there's the client whose address is in a less than desirable neighborhood where you're not comfortable making rounds, yet you hate to turn away business. Stop!

If there's one thing I've learned in my many years of pet sitting, it's to listen to my gut feelings, my instinct, that inner voice, the little radar and just say no!

Think about it. One of the benefits of owning your own business is that you have the power and the right to say "no." You are your own boss and you dictate when, how and for whom you work. Just because you serve the public doesn't mean you have to serve all the people all the time. Not everyone shops at Sears, nor are pet-sitting services suitable for all (for example, aggressive dogs and filthy homes). Even Sears closes its doors occasionally! It has hours you can visit or call the store and hours when you cannot. Most businesses and professions have rules—policies and procedures—that allow them to operate efficiently and effectively.

Professional pet sitters need to make a concerted effort to not sell ourselves short; we need to demand to be treated as the respectable business people that we are. People will take advantage of you—but only if you let them. So, how do you learn to say no? Here are some suggestions for how to go about it in a tactful manner.

- *The last minute caller.* Deter these calls by adding a "last minute" reservation surcharge to your fees. If you're going to accommodate these inconvenient and sometimes inconsiderate customers, make it worth your time! Besides, when you hit the customer in the pocketbook, he often gets the message. If you do not want to accept the last-minute job, simply explain that you're completely booked for the time period. To accept anymore assignments would decrease the amount of time you had contracted for previously scheduled clients. Tell the client that you're sure he can appreciate your position and that you hope he will call you again in the future—but with a little more advance notice! There's nothing wrong with being completely booked—it shows that your services are in demand! And even if you're not booked—this excuse provides a tactful reason to politely say no!

> *Note:* Another suggestion, especially if your office is in your home, is to establish certain office hours for calls and reservations and then stick to them. When it's not office hours, turn the ringer down on your telephone and the sound down on your answering machine. If you accept calls at all hours of the day and night, people will call you at all hours! If you set specific times for calls and announce these to your customers, they will soon adjust and abide by these hours (except for cases of emergency). You must set the rules for your business—and for your customers.

- *The client who tries to get you to come down on your fees.* Politely explain that you are a professional pet sitter and as such, there is more than meets the eye to your services. There are the "hidden" costs of insurance, bonding, advertising, office overhead, taxes, printing, supplies, gas and so on that the client tends to overlook. All the client sees is the visit to his home. When you stand your ground and firmly but tactfully explain this, the client should respect your price setting.

  If he doesn't, remember that your services are not for everyone. As soon as you give a price break, this will turn out to be the job from hell. Sure, some assignments are "easier" than others—but for every easy assignment, there are two more where the fee should be doubled!

- *The client with the aggressive dog.* It's very easy to explain that your company policy prohibits you from sitting for pets that have bitten anyone or acted aggressively in the past. Say you'll be happy to give the caller some names and numbers of area kennels; or say the caller might prefer to ask a family member who is familiar with the dog to provide care. End the call by saying "I'm sorry we can't help you, but thank you for calling."

- *The client in the crime-ridden neighborhood.* Just simply explain that you don't provide sitting services in that zip code area or the western part of town or whatever. Explain that you haven't received enough interest in services from that neighborhood to make it worthwhile to expand your sitting territory to the area. You could offer to take the client's name and number saying if you start a service route in their neighborhood, you will let them know. Don't forget that it's your choice where you pet sit and this is a diplomatic way of saying "no!"

- *The client with the nasty, filthy house.* This can be a little more awkward because you normally won't know the condition of the home until you're actually there for the initial interview. If you are uncomfortable with the assignment after seeing the interior of the home, explain that you don't feel comfortable accepting the assignment and would prefer that the customer make other arrangements for pet care.

  If you're not brave enough to say "no" while face to face with the client, call them immediately upon leaving to explain that you have given it some thought while driving home and think it would be better if they made other arrangements for pet care because you don't feel comfortable with the living/working conditions of the home; then promptly return the house key if you accepted one at the initial interview. Sure, the client may be angry or upset at personal criticism of their housekeeping but better that than a miserable pet-sitting assignment for you! We can't please everyone, and the sooner we learn this, the smarter we'll be!

  Another "out" for this situation was shared by another pet-sitting colleague. She said she simply calls the client, after leaving the home, and explains that she has just realized a conflict with the dates involved that will prevent her from accepting the pet-sitting job.

- *The client who requests extra services, late night visits or something above and beyond your typical services.* Explaining that lawn mowing or house cleaning is not a part of your business should suffice (you

A Filthy Home

I did have a client who, even though she had a master's degree and was a professional in the community, was an extremely poor housekeeper. Boxes of junk were piled from floor to ceiling in several rooms of her house, clothes were everywhere except the closets, and the cats—who probably tired of a seldom clean litter box—used other parts of the home for their bathroom facilities. As you might imagine, it was a very unpleasant situation. The pet sitter assigned to the client was a real cat lover, however, and she felt her visits were the only times these cats were properly cared for and attended to. She opted to wear a face mask to the home (which was, in essence, a large litter box) and sat for this slovenly pet owner for several years. Finally—the client was transferred. We always wondered how in the world she sold her house!

can't blame a person for asking!); however, a referral to these types of services will likely be appreciated by the client.

If you are willing to make an exception and mow the yard or run an errand for a customer, again, make it worth your time! My experience has shown that customers are so glad that you're willing to accommodate their special needs that they will gladly pay your asking price. And, most people know when they're asking for something above and beyond your normal services. Remember that people can't take advantage of you unless you let them!

- *The client who criticizes your services and refuses to pay.* If you pet sit long enough, you're bound to run into this customer eventually. Regardless of the lengths you went to during the assignment, they are determined that you are at fault and they shouldn't have to pay.

  A *personal note here:* I consider myself to be among the most honest, ethical and fair people around. If I was at fault, or if I thought my pet sitter was wrong, I readily admitted it and attempted to make amends with the client. If I thought my pet sitter or I did everything humanly possible to properly fulfill our contract with the client, however, I fought to the bitter end! In other words, once in a while I had to say "No, we won't take or accept your complaints and allegations and we expect our bill to be paid." And I stood by that even if it meant going to small claims court to settle the matter (discussed in Chapter 3).

There are some people and businesses who adhere to the philosophy that the "customer is always right." I have learned that this is not always the case in pet sitting. The customer has the right to have an opinion or to try to get out of paying his bill, but that doesn't make him right!

I hope you'll learn, sooner instead of later, that it is okay to say "no." Standing up for ourselves and our established business policies and practices will create respect and will solidify the professionalism we're creating and commanding for our industry. It will also help you build confidence in yourself and your abilities—plus, it will preserve your sanity and keep pet sitting a career you enjoy!

OTHER POSSIBLE PROBLEMS AND HOW TO HANDLE OR AVOID THEM

The last real disadvantage is something that every business faces eventually—plain old "problems." These come in all shapes and sizes and seem to rear their ugly heads when you least need or want to deal with them. Problems that first come to mind about pet sitting are things like, "What if I am bitten by a dog?" or "What if I lock myself out of a home?"

As I've mentioned before, most of the problems associated with pet sitting can be avoided by using common sense and by doing your homework beforehand. Your homework should include reading the following question-and-answer section, as well as the rest of this book. You also should research and seek out other sources that will help you intelligently and successfully operate your pet-sitting business. As with so many other things, an ounce of prevention is worth a pound of cure.

Q. *What if a pet I'm sitting for is hit by a car?*

A. First, protect yourself by having a clause in your service contract that releases you from that liability if a pet you are sitting for has free access to the outdoors. Cats may disappear for days, and it's very possible they could be injured or killed, or they may disappear permanently. If you're going to care for these free spirits, make sure you're protected with a signed release from liability.

Second, many areas have leash laws that prohibit dogs from running freely. Become familiar with leash laws and pet ordinances that apply to your community. As a reputable pet sitter, you would not want to risk violating such laws. Regardless of whether your area has a leash law, always walk a dog you're caring for on a leash. Point out to owners that they must provide a leash or allow you to supply your own; otherwise, you will not be able to sit for their pets.

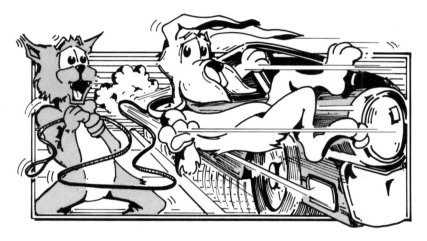

Third, ask the client during your first meeting if the pet is notorious for trying to dash out of a door when someone enters, or if the pet has ever gotten loose on its own. Knowing this history beforehand will help you prevent such problems from occurring. For pets who are prone to escaping out the door, try shaking a plastic market bag at the pet's height as you enter.

By taking these precautions, you will greatly minimize the chances that a pet will be hit by a car, or your liability if such an accident should occur.

Q. *How do I make sure a pet I'm sitting for doesn't run away or get lost?*

A. Be sure to ask clients who have fenced areas for their pets if the enclosed area is secure. Often, dogs will have a favorite spot they dig at, trying to escape. You'll need to know where to look for this spot and how to remedy the situation. With the theft of pets an ongoing concern, you may want to require that all outdoor gates to pet areas be securely locked during the owner's absence. A locked gate will keep neighborhood children away from the pet as well.

It's a smart idea to require that pets you sit for be current on all vaccinations and that they wear a collar with identification if they spend any time out of doors. You should also make notes on your service contract, identifying the breed, sex and age of the pet(s). This information may be helpful in identifying a pet or obtaining medical care, if necessary, while the owner is away.

> *Note:* In addition to the pet's identification tag, many pet sitters now have company identification tags they require each pet under their care to wear. The tags read, "I'm being cared for by XYZ Pet Sitters—999-8877" or "If found, please contact XYZ Pet Sitters—999-8877." This is a great idea because if a pet should escape and be found, the finder would try to call the pet's home phone (usually on the ID tag) and not receive an answer because the owner is away. It's such a simple—but smart—idea that was suggested to me by a colleague. An investment for your business that will give you—and your customers—great peace of mind!

Q. *What if a repairman shows up at a client's home while I'm caring for a pet?*

A. Never let anyone into a client's home unless you have been specifically authorized (in writing on your service contract) to do so by the client; then do so only after the visitor has presented you with satisfactory identification. Even if it's the next-door neighbor wanting to borrow a cup of sugar or someone claiming to be a brother who always borrows the golf clubs, you can be liable. Make it a strict company policy not to let anyone into a client's home other than emergency personnel (such as police, if necessary) and those mentioned by your customer.

Q. *What if a client complains that I forgot to water the plants, as requested?*

A. This is why your service contract is very important. Get all your instructions in writing. It is preferable, by the way, to let the client fill out the contract form. When the client has completed

the form, review it carefully (making sure you can read the handwriting) and add any notations to yourself. By having the client complete the form, you ensure that your job responsibilities are clearly spelled out. If the plants aren't watered, it won't be because you forgot, but because the client failed to ask you to do so. A conscientious pet sitter will notice a room filled with plants and ask the homeowner if they need to be watered. If plants need this care, he or she will note this in the service contract.

> *Note:* As mentioned earlier, plant watering is among the top three reasons that pet sitters have filed insurance claims. If you will be watering a client's plants, make sure no water is spilled on the furniture or hardwood floors, or any other place that may sustain water damage. Also, make sure water faucets are completely turned off before leaving the premises.

Q. *What if a toilet overflows when I try to flush the kitty litter?*

A. Try to get specific instructions from the client about how to dispose of the litter. Never flush the litter unless your client has instructed you in writing to do so. If you are expected to dispose of it in the toilet, ask where the plumber's helper is stored, in the event of a clogged drain. If a toilet does overflow, don't continue to use it. Instead, dispose of the litter in plastic bags to be placed in the outside garbage can.

Note: It is a good idea to ask a client's permission before person- ally using a rest room in a home. Explain that sometimes it is necessary while working and ask if the client would mind (just as you would request permission if you were a guest in someone's home). If the client is agreeable, make sure you leave the toilet as you found it (lid up or down) and that it is not running before you leave the home.

Q. *What if I'm late in getting to a client's home to feed and care for their pets?*

A. This should not happen often because your dependability is the basis of your reputation. However, if you find yourself delayed due to car problems, traffic jams or mischievous critters at another customer's home, use your daily note to tell your client why you were late. Do your best to make sure your next visits are more prompt. Honesty is always the best policy. If you don't explain that you were late one morning, a watchful neighbor probably will inform your client of the fact, and you can expect a complaint.

Q. *What if I notice a urine stain on the carpet?*

A. Always ask your clients how pet accidents should be cleaned in their homes. Even if the client swears the pet is house-trained and that accidents will not occur, get cleaning instructions just in case. Pets often behave differently when their owners are absent, and a change in toilet habits is typically how pets express their loneliness or anger. If you live in an area where inclement weather some- times precludes service rounds from being safely made, you can expect some puddles and messes that will need to be cleaned up.

Q. *How do I handle a pet sitter who tries to sell my clients other services having nothing to do with my business?*

A. As you increase your staff, you will probably find many of your sitters have other jobs. It's important to instruct your sitters that while they are performing their pet-sitting duties, pet sitting should be their primary concern. Sitters should not approach customers for self-serving reasons while they are working for you. When a sitter goes to meet a pet owner, he or she should present your company's business card and talk pets—not real estate or homemade crafts. If the sitter acts more interested in recruiting a client's real estate business than the pet care at hand, the integrity of your service is diminished in the mind of the customer.

Q. *What should I do about clients who return home earlier than anticipated but don't call to discontinue my services?*

A. This lack of consideration causes pet sitters unnecessary trips, and I know of some sitters who have found themselves in embarrassing situations as a result. (One of my sitters arrived at the customer's home for a scheduled 6:45 A.M. visit only to walk in on the client in his underwear making coffee in the kitchen! Needless to say, this was a startling and awkward situation for both parties. The client now calls immediately if he returns home sooner than expected.)

To protect and compensate yourself for these unnecessary trips, have a policy in writing, either in your company's brochure or service contract, covering this situation. My inclination is to hit the client where it hurts (in the pocketbook) and charge full-price for any wasted trips due to his or her negligence and inconsideration. This is reasonable for your time, travel and inconvenience and may prompt the client to remember to call you upon return the next time.

> *Note:* It is a far too common complaint among pet sitters that clients do not notify them of their return, whether it's an early or expected arrival time. To prevent this from becoming a problem in your business, emphasize the necessity for notification upon return to your client during the initial introductory meeting, and point out the monetary penalty (full charges for attempted visits) for failure to do so. A solution that has been received well is to leave a "Client Reminder Card" on your final visit asking the customer to please call your office upon return. Consider having these printed on bright, eye-catching paper. (Similar cards are available for purchase—see the Addenda for ordering information.)

Q. *What do I say to clients who request late night visits for their pets or who want additional services I don't generally perform?*

A. As to the late night visits, that is up to you. It is a company policy that needs to be determined in advance and strictly adhered to. Because the majority of my sitters were women and there was a greater risk of danger for them late at night, I did not offer late night visits to pets. I simply explained this policy to clients, and they have always understood from a liability standpoint. I would much rather clean up pet messes the next morning than risk something happening to one of my staff members. There were only a couple of exceptions made to this rule. They were both instances where the pet required medication at several times of the day and the client was a long-standing customer. We made the visits but charged extra for doing so. Both clients were happy to pay the additional charge and realized that we were bending the rules to accommodate their special needs.

As to providing additional services, this too is something you'll need to consider in advance. If you're willing to comply with special requests, either have an hourly rate established for your help or a per-task fee in mind. If time or liability constraints dictate that you stick strictly to pet-sitting chores, simply explain this to your client. This is why they called you in the first place and they should understand that you aren't a jack of all trades.

Q. *What do I do if a client's teenager or college student appears unexpectedly at one of the homes I'm sitting for and tells me he or she will take over care of the pets?*

A. Never take anyone's word for anything around the home except the person who hired you and signed your contract authorizing services. This person is your employer and the one responsible for your bill. I've heard of too many stories of teenagers or college students who are supposed to be at school or staying with someone. Instead, they sneak home to throw a big party while Mom and Dad are away. This scenario spells trouble. Tell the young person that you'll need to use his phone to call the parents and verify this fact, and speak with the client before ceasing any services.

Q. *How do I prevent clients from calling their assigned sitter at home rather than making reservations through our office as they should?*

A. First, stress to all your sitters the importance of having all reservations made through your office. Point out how it could damage your company's reputation if a client calls only the sitter and leaves a message on an answering machine that services are needed starting immediately. What if the sitter is on vacation or otherwise unavailable? The message would not be received, yet the client would leave assuming service would be provided. Because your office personnel should know which sitters are available and which are not during any time period, all reservations need to come through the proper channel.

When a sitter understands this, he or she can tactfully explain the rationale for your policy that clients must go through the office for reservations. Should a client persist in calling the sitter directly, you'll need to call the customer yourself or write a letter that firmly requests cooperation in this matter. If a client still doesn't comply, then discontinue providing sitting services to this individual.

Another reason you'll want all reservations coming through your office is if you provide liability insurance and a dishonesty bond. For this you'll need an accurate record of all sitting assignments undertaken by your company. If you have no documentation of the job, your insurance company may deny coverage on any claim related to it.

And speaking of insurance, it is vital. You must protect yourself: A pet may be lost or injured while under your care; personal property in a pet owner's home could be damaged or stolen; or other equally unsavory things might occur. One uninsured incident could not only ruin your business but your reputation as well. After clients hear that your insurance may not cover them unless reservations are made through your office, they're usually only too happy to request services this way.

Note: Some pet sitters have started including a phrase in the legal section of their service contract addressing this matter. The clause states something to the effect that "the client understands the necessity and agrees to make future reservations through the pet-sitting company . . ." Because the service contract requires a client's signature, this becomes a written agreement.

It is a legitimate concern that clients and staff pet sitters could try to discretely work together and circumvent the company from being involved in an assignment; however, my experience has shown that this is not a big problem in the industry, for the following reasons:

- If you've done your homework and found good, honest people to work for your company, such dishonest activities will not take place.
- Entrepreneurship is not for everyone. Staff pet sitters, for the large part, are not out to steal your customers—especially if you've required that they sign a non-compete agreement prior to joining your company. Many people like having a supervisor or boss they report to and someone they can count on to support them.
- Pet sitters like the security of knowing they are protected by the company's insurance and dishonesty bond. This is valuable coverage to have and most pet sitters are happy to "play by the rules" in order to have the security it provides.

Discuss these concerns with your attorney. He or she can advise you on steps you can take to keep your customers—and your business—yours.

Q. *What immunizations should a pet sitter require?*

A. Because I am not a veterinarian, I asked my veterinarian what she recommended for pets under my care (you should do the same). I made the suggestions my vet gave me a part of our company policies. The recommended immunizations included:

- Dogs: rabies, coronarvirus, parvovirus
- Cats: rabies, panleukopenia

Although my vet suggested that all vaccines are always recommended for total protection, she said that the preceding ones were the most important for pets receiving in-home care from a professional pet sitter.

When talking with your veterinarian, inquire about zoonotic diseases (those illnesses humans can catch from pets). Some of these include ringworm, scabies, chlamydia, salmonella, cat scratch fever, Lyme disease, Rocky Mountain Spotted Fever, roundworms and rabies. Find out how you can avoid transmission of these diseases and their symptoms. Check with your local health department about rabies vaccinations for you and your pet sitters. It's also a good idea for people who work with pets to remain up-to-date with tetanus vaccinations. And be aware that cat bites can be very serious. Because of the way cats lick and clean themselves, they have a lot of bacteria in their saliva. This bacteria can be transmitted easily to humans through a bite. Should you or any staff members be bitten by a cat, it's wise to seek medical attention.

Q. *My business has been open for six months and some days the phone doesn't ring. How long does it take to build a pet-sitting business and start making money?*

A. This depends upon several variables, such as location, perseverance, advertising and so on, which were discussed in detail in Chapter 5. However, when someone calls or writes to ask me this question (someone who is usually having a down day), I always ask "What have you done *today* to make your business a success? What did you do yesterday? What do you plan to do tomorrow?" Success does not just miraculously happen in any business—it takes work and determination. Although you have a great idea with a pet-sitting business and may be the smartest person in the world, you have to constantly work at selling your services. My advice is to try to do one thing each day that will help your business to grow. Things you should try include:

- Distributing doorknob hangers in neighborhoods

- Visiting pet stores, groomers or vet offices with business cards and something sweet for their morning or afternoon coffee break

- Dropping by doctor or dentist offices to see if you can leave some of your company newsletters as reading material in the waiting room

- Calling apartment complexes to see if they allow pets and if so, if they would allow you to post a brochure or distribute door-knob hangers that advertise your services

The list goes on and on. There are so many opportunities to educate, inform, advertise and publicize your at-home pet care services. Seize every opportunity you can. Assertiveness is required to keep your phone ringing!

As for showing a profit and making money in this business, it was not until my third year of business that this began to happen for me. I've also heard from other pet sitters that the third year seems to be the magic number. However, with the wealth of information in this book and the numerous resources available to today's pet-sitting entrepreneur, I think profits can be realized sooner for an industrious and determined pet sitter.

Q. *What about clients who want you to visit their cat every other day or who ask you to feed the dog but ignore the cat (not charge) because they will leave plenty of food and water?*

A. Daily visits are something else you'll be wise to discuss with your veterinarian. I think most veterinarians will recommend that pets be visited at least once a day—especially cats. Urinary blockages or other illnesses could be fatal for a cat that doesn't receive prompt medical attention. Besides, pets need love and personal attention, and it is this part of our services that makes pet sitting so popular. Determine what your visitation policy will be in advance. If any exceptions are made to the policy, make sure the circumstances are noted in writing on your service contract.

For the client who asks that you ignore the cat, simply explain or put it in writing on your company literature that your conscience would not allow you to overlook a cat in need of food, medical care or human attention—so please don't request that the care of household felines be neglected!

THE BEST FROM THE BEST—TIPS FROM THE FIELD

As mentioned earlier, I have learned so much from networking with other pet sitters through my many years in this business. Here are some tips I've picked up along the way that I'm sure will be helpful to you as a pet sitter. They are in no particular order or sequence; each is as important as the other.

- Carry an identification card in your wallet that states you're a professional pet sitter. List on the card a person who should be contacted to take over pet care visits in the event of your being injured or ill.

- Ring the doorbell before entering homes just in case the client has unexpectedly arrived home early.

- Pet owners should always be alerted to any problem you have, whether or not you think it's significant. Don't worry about bothering or disturbing them—pets and homes are important to people!

- Never discuss clients and their travel plans over cellular and cordless phones because they might be monitored or overheard on other cordless phones or on scanner radio frequencies.

- Invest in a Polaroid camera for your business. Take a photo of each pet for your files. A photo helps if a pet becomes lost and serves as documentation should any damage occur.

- Don't place stacked mail where it can be viewed through a window. This is an indication that no one is home! If your client plans on checking his or her answering machine or voice mail while away, call and leave the client updates as to how the pets are doing. Clients appreciate this caring touch! Bring any deliveries (UPS, water jugs and so on) inside the home, or request a different delivery date.

- Use a lead pencil on any ornery keys—makes them work like new!

- Make notes on vehicles left in the client's driveway, such as make, model, license plate number and color. This information will be useful during the owner's absence in the event of a theft.

- Carry some jugs of water in your trunk. These may come in handy if you discover any frozen pipes in a client's home.

- If it's too hot to take a dog for a walk and your client has a swimming pool, take the dog for a swim! Obtain permission from your client before doing so.

- Keep a collapsible pet carrier and a pillowcase in your trunk. These things may be useful to transport a sick or injured cat or dog.

- In the event of the death of a client's pet, send a pet sympathy card and/or make a contribution in the pet's name.

- Pill crushers are a handy item for pets requiring medication; however, always check with the pet's vet prior to crushing any pills. Dispensing the crushed pill in a teaspoon of baby food (meat varieties) usually makes the task easier with cats and dogs. (Be sure to ask the vet if the pet has any food allergies.)

- Make your driving time productive. Keep a car phone, books on tape, along with a notebook and pen handy for use while driving or stuck in traffic jams.

- When testing a house key at the introductory interview, try to open the door after it has been closed and locked.

- Ignore possible temptations to use a client's swimming pool, exercise equipment, television or stereo, computer and so on.

- Clip pet food coupons and leave them in the homes of clients who use that brand of food.

- For clients who have burglar alarms on their homes, remember that the alarm company has a record of when the alarm is turned on and off. Some clients will use this record to ascertain the length of their pet-sitting visits!

CHAPTER 8

USEFUL BUSINESS FORMS

Professional, effective business forms are extremely important to any reputable pet-sitting service. A comprehensive form can save you valuable time, streamline your company procedures, protect your assets and enhance your company's image. You'll be wise to devote your attention, energies and money to developing forms that will best benefit your service.

In this chapter, I will give you an overview of the forms most highly recommended for a pet sitter and discuss some of their necessary components. Because a service contract will probably be your most important document, let's begin our discussion with it.

DESIGNING A SERVICE CONTRACT

You will use this form to gather information about each assignment; it will also serve as your legal agreement to perform pet-sitting services for a client on his or her premises. I highly recommend you consult with an attorney before using any contract you have written or purchased to ensure that it adequately protects you. Regardless, the following advice should help you prepare a rough draft or mock-up to review with your attorney.

Client Information

The service contract can be divided into sections. The first section allows you to gather information about the client. You'll need spaces for the client's name, address, home and business phone numbers. You'll want to know the date the customer is leaving town and when he or she anticipates returning. There should be room for the client to write where he or she can be reached (address and telephone number). You should find out the name of a local friend, family member or neighbor to contact in the event of an emergency, if you are unable to reach the client. After all, people on vacation do not sit in their rooms waiting for their pet sitter to call. If a home under your care is burglarized, the pet sitter probably won't know about valuables in the home that may be missing, something law enforcement officers would need to know. Having a close friend or family member to call on may help in such a situation.

Other Keys

You should list on your service contract who else has a key to the home. This list can be part of the first section. There are several reasons why this is important. If the home is burglarized, the pet sitter will be able to provide the police with a list of key holders, which would aid in the investigation. Also, occasionally a client will have his or her home for sale without displaying a FOR SALE sign. The sitter may arrive to care for a pet and find a real estate agent and family of four walking through the home. Hopefully, reading this question on your service contract will remind the client to inform the sitter that a real estate agent has house keys. Finally, if a pet sitter does the unthinkable and locks herself out of the house, it's nice to know the neighbor three doors away also has a key.

Natural Circumstances

If you live in an area of inclement weather or natural disasters, hopefully you have prepared a formal disaster plan for your business. You should also have a written Plan B of action on your contract. Natural circumstances beyond your control may make it hazardous or impossible to make your pet-sitting visits. Having the name and number of a client's nearby neighbor may be a crucial part of Plan B.

Pet Information

The next portion of your contract should deal with the information you need to have about the pets. There are several things you'll want to include on your service contract: the pet's name, type, breed, sex, age, diet, medication and exercise requirements. Leave enough room so you can make notations to yourself, such as "Taffy is the white cat, and Samantha is the Siamese." It's important to have good notations; if you're sitting for several different clients on the same days, it can be easy to get instructions or pets confused.

Obtain the pet's medical history on your service contract. The little Chihuahua having seizures on your morning visit will throw you into a panic, unless you know this is normal for the dog and that rushing it to the vet isn't necessary. But if the seizures are not normal, you need to have the client's veterinarian's name and telephone number at hand. You should also obtain permission from the client to seek medical attention for his or her pet.

Something you may not think of asking is where the client stores the pet food. Not everyone keeps it in the same place. I've found it stored in pantries, garage trash cans and bathroom closets; I've found it in containers on top of a refrigerator. Rarely is it stored in what you may consider to be a logical place. Save yourself time and a potential problem by learning this in advance.

You should also know if the pet is allowed treats. Many owners are counting their pets' calories these days, and you don't want to sabotage any diets by offering treats.

Last but certainly not least, ask if the pet has any favorite forms of affection or exercise. If it loves to have its ears scratched or to chase a Frisbee, you want to know in order to make the most of the quality time you'll be spending with the pet. Find out what you can do to make the pet feel loved and happy during the owner's absence. It's this personalized part of your service that makes it so unique and appealing, and it's why the client most likely called you in the first place. Make sure you deliver lots of tender loving care.

Household Routines

The third section of your service contract should address pertinent information regarding the client's home. Spell out any additional household services you're willing to provide, and the extra fee for each chore. You or the client can simply check off what he or she would like done—the newspaper and mail brought inside, the lights alternated, the plants watered and so on.

You might ask if the client wants the radio or television left on during his or her absence. This is a good crime deterrent, because it provides noise and the impression of activity inside the home. It also provides companionship for some pets.

It's also a good idea to ask if the client wants his or her telephone answered. This was something I had not anticipated when I first began pet sitting. I found it was a strange feeling to be in someone's home and hear the phone ring and ring. I suppose it's almost a natural reflex or habit to want to answer a ringing phone! Shortly after this experience, there was an article in my local newspaper about a theft ring that had recently been caught in the act. The thieves had been calling homes and, if there was no answer, they would go to the home. Learning about this ingenious little scheme was all I needed to begin asking my customers if they wanted their telephone answered. Some customers feel it isn't necessary, while others appreciate the attention to detail this offer shows. When I am expected to answer the phone, I always act as if I am a full-time house sitter staying in the home. Should the caller be someone unscrupulous, this will hopefully prevent any wrongdoing. To date, though, it has always been a friendly voice on the other end of the telephone line. Of course, I always leave the customer a message with the caller's name and number, as well as the date and time of the call.

Note: With the popularity of answering machines today, a client may tell you just to let his or her machine take care of all calls. It's wise to ask the customer if she will be checking messages during her absence from home. If the answer is yes, and you need to let the client know something that's not quite important enough for a long-distance call, you can leave a message on the answering machine. An example might be: "This is Jane, your XYZ Pet Sitter. Just wanted to let you know that we had an unexpected snowfall last night with about eight inches accumulation. Due to the record cold temperatures and snow, I brought your dogs into the basement to weather out the evening more comfortably. If there's any problem with leaving them inside during the evenings until it warms up some, please call me at home: 999-2403. Thank you." And, even if there's nothing newsworthy to report, it's still a nice idea to call and leave a message letting the client know everything is going well and that you hope they are having a good trip.

Extra Services

You should allow enough space in the third section of your service contract for notes about any extra services that may be requested. These will be tasks above and beyond your normal responsibilities; if you're willing to perform them, you will need to negotiate fees while meeting with the client. Examples that come to mind from my own experience include watering a client's greenhouse full of plants. Although my service normally allows for the watering of a few household plants, this particular client, an avid horticulturist, was asking for more. Although I was happy to be able to help her by looking after the greenhouse, I did have to charge a considerable amount for the extra time. (I also had her sign a statement that said I would not be liable if any of her plants died—I truly am not a green thumb!)

Another client inquired if his dry cleaning could be picked up. One family, who would be returning late at night after a three-week trip to Europe, asked if some breakfast groceries could be left in their refrigerator. One of the funniest requests was to "feed the bread." Making sourdough bread requires keeping a starter base in the refrigerator and "feeding" it every few days with a couple of ingredients such as potato flakes. This particular client said she felt like an idiot making the request but, needless to say, she was relieved and thrilled to learn I would do this for her while looking after her poodles. It only took a minute or two to add the ingredients, so I didn't even charge her extra. Upon her return, a freshly baked loaf of this wonderful bread was on her kitchen table as a gift for me! Sometimes it pays to be nice. When discussing extras with clients, keep in mind that most people know if their requests are beyond the scope of your normal services. Usually they are more than happy to pay extra for special requests. So, don't let a customer try to take advantage of you; fortunately this probably won't be attempted very often.

Returning House Keys

How you return a customer's house keys should be clarified on your service contract. Returning a key personally may be the preferable way, because it gives you and the client peace of mind knowing the key got to the rightful owner. This visit also prompts the customer to pay you for your services at that time and often will get you a tip as well. However, it does take additional time and travel to return house keys, so make sure your pet-sitting fees can absorb these costs, or consider charging a nominal amount for key return. As noted in an earlier chapter, many homes these days have dead-bolt locks that require a key to lock them. Thus, these keys have to be personally returned anyway.

> *Note:* Beware of the client (one without dead-bolt locks) who instructs you to leave the key on the kitchen counter and lock yourself out of the home after your final visit. This would be fine except that flights are missed or delayed, cars break down and inclement weather may make it impossible for the owner to return when anticipated. If the key has been locked inside the home, an expensive locksmith will be necessary for you to continue caring for the pets and home. A word to the wise: agree to leave the key well hidden outside for the client if he or she does not want it personally returned. This way, you still have access to the home should it be necessary.

Of course there will be many clients who just adore your service and use it frequently. They will eventually request that you simply retain a key until further notice (see "Always Ready" Service, discussed in Chapter 3).

This is the ultimate compliment and preferred procedure but remember, retaining house keys permanently increases your liability. Discuss this aspect with your insurance agent and attorney and do be sure to safeguard clients' keys at all times.

Fees and Hours

It's important to have your established fees and normal route hours listed on your service contract, so everything is clearly spelled out. However, some pet sitters prefer to have a separate fee schedule as an addendum to their business literature. The rationale is that if fees change, the whole service contract does not have to be reprinted. Regardless of the procedure you choose, make sure there is a place on your contract to fill in what the client's total fee will be. This should be understood and agreed upon before your services begin.

You should also consider noting on your service contract whether any type of cancellation fee applies and under what circumstances. If something prevents a customer's trip from taking place, you still have to consider the time and travel pet sitters have invested in initial interviews, as well as the fact that your service was planning on this job as a source of revenue.

Another policy that may be important to list on your service contract is whether you have a one-time-only visit charge. An example of this would be the client who is going to a nearby town for a football game. He expects to return home later on that same day and only needs one suppertime visit made to feed and exercise his dog. Unless your fee is a bit higher for these types of visits, they're probably not worth the time and effort of initial interviews and returning house keys.

Legal Considerations

The last part of a service contract should contain the clause(s) that will explain exactly who is responsible for what regarding terms and conditions of this agreement. Making sure your service contract adequately protects you and makes your client feel comfortable is a delicate matter; it probably requires the advice and direction of an attorney. You want to be absolutely sure your service contract will be a binding agreement. When meeting with your attorney to draw up the contract, consider addressing the following questions:

1. When and how must the customer pay for rendered services?

2. Who is responsible for the veterinarian's fees if such assistance becomes necessary during the owner's absence?

3. Who is responsible for extra time expended by a pet sitter due to emergencies regarding the pet or home?

4. Who is responsible for purchases—such as additional cat litter or paper towels—necessary for the satisfactory performance of duties?

5. Under what, if any, circumstances can you or your company be held liable during the duration of the contract?

6. Under what, if any, circumstances will the client be held liable during the duration of the contract?

7. When do the terms of the contract actually begin and end?

8. If other people will have access to the home at the same time you do, will the client release you from liability for any damage that could result from the other parties' negligence?

As you can see from the implications these questions bring to mind, having an inclusive service contract is extremely important. Although structuring this part of your contract may seem overwhelming, don't let it frighten you or prevent you from getting into the wonderful world of pet sitting. Just take your time, think through all of these points, hash them out with objective friends or family members, then visit a good attorney for his or her advice and appropriate direction. For those readers who don't relish the idea of designing a service contract, there are now standard pet-sitting service contracts available for purchase (see the Addenda for ordering information). Whether you buy a service contract or create your own, consider a thorough and professional service contract to be a one-time investment that will guide you well in the years to come.

Note: The legally binding aspects of a service contract are the signatures of the parties involved, so be sure your service contract has a signature line for the client and pet sitter and a place for the date the contract was entered into. Make sure you obtain the client's signature on this critical document!

INVOICE

Some pet sitters give the client a copy of the service contract that lists the total amount due, and this serves as the customer's invoice. This procedure cuts down on accounting and postage costs. However, some clients don't realize that the service contract is their invoice, and they often have to be reminded of the payment procedure several times.

Other pet sitters have a separate invoice that they use for billing. Some design this form themselves on a computer and have it preprinted with their company name, address and logo; others purchase a basic invoice from an office supply store and personalize it with a rubber stamp.

Whichever method you choose for your business, an invoice is a fairly basic and simple form. It usually includes an invoice number, a description of what the bill is for and the date when payment is due. Although not necessary, it's a nice gesture to include a self-addressed envelope with the invoice for the customer's convenience when paying.

> *Note:* Some pet sitters place postage on the self-addressed envelopes they leave for payment; however, I think this is an unnecessary gesture. After all, how many bills do you receive that include a stamped self-addressed envelope? Postage is expensive; however, the pet sitters who do this tell me they receive payment promptly so the extra expense is worth it to them.

DAILY LOG

As stated earlier, it's my opinion that every professional and reputable pet-sitting service needs some kind of daily log form. Some pet sitters simply use a scratch pad for writing the daily report for the client; others have professionally printed forms for these notes; still others use a checklist and mark off daily tasks as they are completed (notes can be made at the bottom of this form, if the pet sitter observes anything of interest to the client).

Your own ideas and creativity may lead you to design a totally different type of daily log to meet the needs of your pet-sitting service, or you may prefer to purchase the camera-ready "Daily Diary" forms that are available (see the Addenda for ordering information). In any event, I encourage you to make some kind of daily log an integral part of your service.

EVALUATION FORM

The value of this type of form to you as a business owner is immeasurable. It allows clients the chance to give you feedback that will keep your services on target and progressive. A well-designed evaluation form will help you assess what aspects of your services are well received and who is doing the best job delivering those services. After all, if you have a staff of pet sitters, they most likely work independently without direct supervision. You need some way of knowing the job they are doing as representatives of your company. An evaluation form will provide this information.

Although some clients will not take the time to fill out and return such a form, many of them will be impressed and complimented that their opinion matters and will eagerly respond. My clients were very helpful in returning this form, and some made suggestions that improved our services.

I know of some pet sitters who leave a report card type of evaluation that allows the client to grade the sitter's performance and note the customer's degree of satisfaction with services rendered. Others go into more detail, asking the client specific questions, such as "Did the pet sitter arrive in a timely manner?"; "Was the pet sitter conscientious and caring?"; or "Were your instructions followed?"

Another extremely important function of this form is that it permits you to ask clients how they first heard about your pet-sitting service. These replies can clue you in to what advertising is bringing you results. And with the high cost of advertising, you do want to know where you're getting the most for your buck.

I insisted that my pet sitters leave a self-addressed evaluation form on their last visit to a customer's home. The recourse this form allows our clients gives them a comfortable feeling about the professionalism of our service. And, should a client not return an evaluation form, it's a good idea to follow up with a telephone call to ascertain that the client was pleased with your services.

CLIENT RESERVATION FORM

This is the form you'll use to schedule reservations and maintain basic information on each customer. It can be as simple as the "Customer Card" discussed in Chapter 3, or you may want to expand it to an $8^1/2$" x 11" sheet or keep a more extensive client record in your computer.

The client reservation form needs to be something that is easily accessible to you when taking phone reservations for services. It will provide you with basic information at a glance, such as address, pet names, last dates of service, assigned pet sitter and so on. When you can speak more familiarly with a client, their comfort level increases—plus, they are impressed at your attention to detail!

Client reservation forms should include a space for special notations about a customer's needs (for example, Mr. Smith's dogs love carrots as treats). It also is helpful to include a column for customer payments and dates of payments. As discussed in Chapter 3, this system can quickly tell you which accounts are delinquent.

NOTIFICATION FORMS

These are forms that pet sitters, in recent years, have found to be extremely beneficial. There are three kinds of notification forms, which are described in the following list:

- *Vet Notification.* This is a form, or postcard, that states the customer's pet(s) will be under the care of your pet-sitting service for a certain time period. The client's signature on this form authorizes the veterinarian to administer medical care, as needed, during the owner's absence. This signed authorization also assures the vet that he or she will be paid by the customer (sometimes a monetary amount is specified) for medical attention. Vet offices usually make this form a permanent part of the customer's file.

- *Neighbor Notification.* This form, or postcard, notifies neighbors that personnel from your pet-sitting service will be caring for their neighbor's pet(s) during a specified time period. It should list a phone number where neighbors can reach you, if necessary, and it's helpful to list the car make and model the neighbor can expect to see visiting the home. With so much concern about crime and the popularity of neighborhood crime-stop programs, watchful neighbors will be glad to know that your service is authorized to be on their neighbor's premises. And you'll be glad that neighbors aren't calling law enforcement officials to investigate your presence in the neighborhood!

- *Police/Sheriff Notification.* This form, letter or postcard informs the appropriate law enforcement agency that your service is authorized to visit the premises of the customer at the specified address during the specified time period. This notification alerts the agency that the client will be out of town (thus they may step up patrol of the area) and familiarizes them with your service. Should you ever need to report a burglary or problem at a client's home, it will be helpful if the law enforcement agency is aware of your business and reputation.

Notification forms also serve another important function. They advertise your service to the recipient. Neighbors may be more likely to call you for pet care when they know other people who use your services. Vets may be more likely to recommend your services after they see how many of their customers entrust their pet(s) to you. Law enforcement personnel may recommend you as a form of crime deterrence when they see how often the public relies upon your service for in-home pet care.

ADDITIONAL FORMS

The forms already discussed are probably the most basic for a professional pet sitter just starting out. However, as you discuss liabilities with your insurance agent and attorney, there may be strong arguments for the development of other pertinent business forms. For example, one sitting service I know has all clients fill out and sign a form that dictates their wishes in the event of their pet's death during the sitting assignment. Another has a separate form that pertains to the safekeeping and liabilities associated with the client's house keys. A third service has a more detailed form that deals with the health history and habits of each pet. A fourth utilizes an emergency repair form in case they encounter broken water pipes or other household emergency. While some forms—such as a client information card, service contract and brochure—are found in all pet-sitting businesses, others are developed to meet the personal needs of each service.

Of course, as your business grows, you'll need such forms as employment application forms. Standard employment applications can be purchased in most office supply stores, but they are rudimentary in nature. With the unique demands of pet sitting, a more comprehensive employment application form is required to help you determine which candidates are best suited for your openings. With time, you'll soon know the questions to ask job applicants and will be able to design your own application or alter a store-bought form accordingly. To avoid violating any state or federal hiring laws, it's advisable to consult with an attorney about any employment application you use in your business.

TIPS FROM PET SITTERS

Some tips about business forms from other pet sitters include the following:

- Be sure to ask on your service contract if the dog knows any commands. This information can come in handy when you're trying to get a dog to sit or stop jumping on you!

- Ask clients for the date of their pets' birthdays; then, surprise them with a pet birthday card or gift. Clients will love your thoughtfulness!

- If your clients are flying while traveling, find out the airline and flight number and write it on your service contract. Although airline crashes are rare, it's useful information to have on hand if one should occur or if you simply want to make sure a client's flight is on time for a return home.

- Set aside a section on the front of your business envelopes where you can write a personalized note or greeting to the household pet. This is a humorous and personal touch!

CHAPTER 9

CLOSING YOUR BUSINESS

With proper planning it is possible to have a long and rewarding career in professional pet sitting. However, sometimes circumstances (family needs, job transfers, retirement, burnout) require that you get out of the business. When it's time to say good-bye to this career, you most likely will have two options: closing the business or selling it. Hopefully, the investment you have made in starting and growing your pet-sitting service will be something you can sell to realize a nice financial return. If you're making money as a pet sitter, you don't just want to close the doors and quit. The business you have built may be worth more than you think.

Keep in mind that selling a service business is a little different than selling a retail outlet or product-oriented venture. With the latter, you most likely have inventory, a building or a lease for business space, fixtures, equipment as well as a business name, reputation and goodwill. In a service business, such as pet sitting, there are more intangible assets. You probably have a trademarked name, established operating procedures and forms, a client list, and your reputation and goodwill. Although reputation and goodwill are extremely important assets, their value is often harder to establish than the value of a building or retail inventory.

If you've intentionally kept your pet-sitting service small and worked out of your home, you most likely have only your client list to sell. With the growth of the pet-sitting industry, this is becoming a more frequent occurrence. What typically happens is that another area pet sitter or pet-sitting firm buys the client list for either a set amount per name or a percentage of business revenues realized from the customer over the next year or other set period. In the case of the percentage method, the purchasing pet sitter usually makes a down payment and then makes the final payment at the end of the specified term. The selling pet sitter usually notifies customers in writing about the sale of the client list, recommends the new pet-sitting service, and thanks the client for their past business. Some closing pet sitters even take the purchasing pet sitter around to personally introduce them to clients and their pets. Although an outright purchase of a client list (so much per name) results in a faster up-front payment, the percentage procedure can eventually result in a higher price for the seller. Discuss these options with your accountant and attorney.

If you have built a thriving and lucrative pet-sitting business, talk first with your accountant before starting the selling process. See if he or she can help you set a value on your business and discuss tax ramifications of selling for a lump sum versus on installment. Determine in advance if you can afford to finance any of the selling price. There could be a person well-suited for your business who is interested but who doesn't have all the cash readily available. (I know of some staff pet sitters who have bought the business from the owner when the opportunity presented itself. The owners were confident in selling to them and financing part of the sale because they knew the work ethics of these employees.)

HOW A BUSINESS BROKER CAN ASSIST

When you're thinking of selling, it's also a good idea to talk with a business broker. Ask your accountant for a recommendation or check your local Yellow Pages for listings. Business brokers sell businesses every day, and they may have someone in mind who would be a strong candidate to buy your business. A business broker also can help you determine an asking price or confirm the figure you and your accountant have come up with. Additional benefits of using a business broker are the convenience and confidentiality they provide. A business broker can run a blind ad, screen potential candidates and arrange for personal meetings with you only when the candidate seems like a good prospect. Find out at the outset what the business broker's fees are and try to find one who charges only when a sale goes through.

A business broker can advise you about what financial information you'll need to provide. This will include past tax returns, profit and loss statements, equipment and asset lists, lease agreements and so on. If a buyer wants to make an offer for your business, the broker, as an objective third party, can keep personalities from damaging a prospective sale. Once a price and terms are agreed upon, the broker can prepare a buy-and-sell agreement; then attorneys and accountants will become involved to work out the final details. If you decide to list your business with a business broker, be prepared to give him an exclusive right-to-sell contract for at least six months. Buying a business is a major decision; it usually takes some time to find the right buyer.

Selling my pet-sitting business was an emotion-packed experience. Although my mind knew it was the right thing to do, my heart was having second thoughts. I had poured so much of myself into building the business that it was, in many respects, like my child. Could I really let go? Yet, when the attorney handed me my check at the closing it was a very exhilarating feeling—it's very rewarding to realize the fruits of your labor!

Keep in mind while contemplating your pet-sitting business and while running and building it, that the decisions and actions you take and make will ultimately affect the final outcome of your business. Whether you ultimately leave the business to your children or sell it, you want to have built something of value that has brought you pleasure—and pride.

PS AND QS OF SAYING GOOD-BYE

Just as there are steps to take when starting a pet-sitting business, there is protocol to follow when closing or leaving your business. Remember how excited you were about starting your pet-sitting service and how you wanted to do everything the right way in order to be a success—and a credit—to the industry. Let that same philosophy guide you as you leave the profession. Steps to take include:

- Notify your customers of your decision to sell or close the business. Inform them of their future options for in-home pet care. Specify how the return of house keys will be handled.

- When returning client house keys, have the customer sign an acknowledgement that their key has been returned.

- Notify your business insurance and bond provider of the change in ownership or closing of business.

- Notify any professional affiliations, such as Pet Sitters International or your local Chamber of Commerce, of the change in ownership or closing of business. Otherwise, you may still continue to receive referrals from the Pet Sitters International Locator Line. This could be annoying as well as an embarrassment to the organization that is giving out incorrect information.

- Offer to provide letters of recommendation for staff members who may be losing their position due to your closing or sale of the business.

- Talk with your accountant and attorney to make sure the proper documentation has been filed with your city or state regarding the sale of your business or closing of your corporation.

Although selling or leaving the business may be the last thing on your mind as you ponder getting into pet sitting, I have included the subject in this edition because the industry has evolved to the point that the sale of pet-sitting businesses is becoming commonplace. You may prefer to investigate the possibility of buying an existing pet-sitting business rather than starting your own. Sometimes it can be more economical to purchase a business instead of starting from scratch. If you're thinking of selling or buying a business, there is now a publication available, "Selling Your Pet Sitting Business," written by my respected colleague, Bill Foster (see the Addenda for ordering information). Whether you're buying or selling a pet-sitting business, be sure to seek advice from your accountant and attorney.

CHAPTER 10

IN CONCLUSION

TRACKING YOUR GROWTH

You will find it helpful to chart such things as the number of daily inquiries received about your service or the actual number of bookings or assignments per month, per holiday, per zip code and so on. This can be charted by making check marks on a calendar or map, or by keeping a log of customer names by various categories. Of course, a computer can simplify these statistical tasks! Such records are important to review on a regular basis to help you plan and set goals for your business. Plus, there will be a discouraging day every now and then, and it's reassuring to refer to these statistics to see how you've grown since last Easter or Labor Day.

Keeping these types of records will also help you learn the busiest areas and times for your business. Knowing this will assist you in staffing appropriately and scheduling the best time for your own vacation.

BUSINESS TRENDS

Although my business grew to the point that business was steady year-round, slow periods do occur and are to be expected. Fortunately, the city in which my pet-sitting service was located is only a couple of hours away from the coast to the east and the mountains to the west. These close vacation spots provided me with winter business from skiers as well as year-round business from area beach buffs.

I found my busiest season began with Easter and continued through Labor Day. This is the traditional family vacation period and has the nicest weather. September and October were also good months for us due to many clients who went on fall fishing trips, foliage tours and those who preferred to vacation when the kids were back in school. November brought lots of Thanksgiving reservations, and Christmas was absolutely the busiest holiday of all. The slower months were January, February and March, probably due to people rebounding from holiday spending, computing their taxes, or just plain nesting in bad weather. I always used the slower months to recuperate from the busy season, clean files and catch up on paper work. I also tried to get away to some warm, sunny destination!

My experience has shown that people travel for many reasons: business, pleasure and often because of family emergencies. Some people prefer a January vacation, while others always vacation the third week of July. There is no rule of thumb for when people travel. The good side to this is you'll find that your pet-sitting services are needed throughout the year. The downside to this is that there's no sure way to predict the amount of business you'll do each month, and this, at times, can be frustrating.

Don't be surprised to find your services in demand even when the client is not leaving home. Sometimes pet owners will need your help due to an illness or injury that prevents them from properly caring for their pets. I recall several new mothers, overwhelmed with demands of a baby, who called to request pet-care services. They couldn't juggle new baby needs with necessary dog walks and pet care! Other times, long working hours may prompt a pet owner to request your services. And some dog owners, kept busy at work, will want a monthly contract with you to walk and exercise their pooches at lunchtime each day. Midday dog walking has become the bread and butter of many pet-sitting services in large metropolitan areas. It's a good idea to advertise your services as useful for the "in-town" pet owner as well as to those who must travel. This may increase your volume of business.

CRIME DETERRENCE

Another business trend has occurred due to the level of crime in today's society. Many pet sitters market the added benefit of crime deterrence that home visits provide; this has resulted in requests for house checks from people who don't even own a pet. These clients simply like the crime-deterrent services of newspaper and mail pickup, plant watering and light rotation. You may want to emphasize this aspect of your pet-sitting services in your advertising.

OVERNIGHT PET AND HOUSE SITTING

Another trend growing in popularity is that of overnight pet-sitting services. Some clients, whose pets are used to sharing their owner's bed, prefer that someone actually stay overnight in their home to provide this additional companionship for their beloved pet. Others like the additional crime deterrence provided by someone living in the home. Additional time, liabilities and rules are involved when a pet-sitting service provides sleepover services. Give careful thought to adding such services; the following questions are just some of the issues to be considered:

- What hours will the pet sitter be required to stay in the home?
- Will the customer or pet sitter provide food for meals?
- What is the pet sitter allowed to use in the home, for example TV, microwave, stereo and so on?
- Can the pet sitter entertain guests while living in a customer's home?

As you can see by these questions, overnight pet sitting involves a different set of variables. More than likely, you'll need a separate service contract for overnight pet-/house-sitting assignments. However, for the pet-sitting service that can provide reliable, caring and trustworthy sitters who are bonded, insured and security-checked to provide overnight care, there is lots of potential business out there.

EXPANDED SERVICES

One other trend our industry is experiencing is that of add-on services. These include working with mobile groomers to provide in-home grooming services, delivery of premium pet foods to busy client homes and, as mentioned earlier, pet transportation services to vet appointments or groomers for working pet owners. The positive reception to these additional services is further proof of the love affair Americans are having with their pets!

SOME CLOSING THOUGHTS

Every successful endeavor begins with one small step. By purchasing and reading this book, you've taken that first small step toward opening your own successful business.

Pet sitting has provided me with an enjoyable, challenging and rewarding career. As I have mentioned, there was little information available to guide me when I began pet sitting. I had to work long and hard to develop a successful business and elevate pet sitting to a recognized, respectable and credible livelihood. Now that pet sitting has become an established industry, the demand for at-home pet care is only going to grow as pet owners learn of the advantages and conveniences it offers. Tremendous potential exists for the pet sitter who is willing to work hard to operate a reputable and professional pet-sitting service.

It's now up to you. Pet sitting is an exciting, interesting, fun business that requires a relatively low up-front investment. The need for this service exists in large and small communities—and it can be met with your sincere and energetic commitment to provide the best in personalized home pet care. Remember that the pioneers in this field are counting on you to uphold and continue the standards of excellence that are necessary for successful pet sitters. Hopefully, this book will make meeting this requirement much easier for future pet sitters everywhere.

CHAPTER 11

ADDENDA

ESTIMATED START-UP COSTS AND CHECKLIST

Business License(s) _____

Name Registration _____

Attorney Fees _____

Legal Structure Costs _____
    (partnership agreement, incorporation and so on)

Accountant Fees _____

Liability Insurance _____

Dishonesty Bond _____

Deposit for Office Space _____

Rent for Office Space _____

Moving Expenses for Office Site Set-Up _____

Bank Charges _____

Business Telephone Deposit _____

Business Telephone Installation _____

Monthly Charge for Business Telephone _____

Telephone (Purchase or Rental) _____

Answering Machine and/or _____
       Personal Answering Service _____

Cellular Phone and/or _____
      Pager _____

Calculator _____

Typewriter and/or
    Computer and Software   _____

Desk   _____

Chair   _____

File Cabinet   _____

Shelf or Bookcase   _____

Business Form Design   _____

Business Form Printing   _____

Basic Office Supplies   _____

Pet-Sitting Supplies   _____

Office Library Books and Videos   _____

Advertising

    Newspaper   _____

    Yellow Pages   _____

    Radio   _____

    Television   _____

    Local Publications   _____

    Other   _____

Annual Dues for Professional Affiliations and Subscriptions

    Pet Sitters International   _____

    Chamber of Commerce   _____

    Pet-Related Organizations   _____

    Better Business Bureau   _____

Reference Books

    Business-related   _____

    Pet-related   _____

    Other   _____

Magazine Subscriptions

    Business-related   _____

    Pet-related   _____

    Other   _____

Miscellaneous

    _____   _____

    _____   _____

Total   _____

HELPFUL PRODUCTS FOR PROFESSIONAL PET SITTERS

As stated at the outset, much of what I have learned about the pet-sitting business has been through trial and error. It has been my intent, in writing this book, to save other prospective pet sitters some of the hassle, headaches and money I went through in establishing and successfully operating my own business. Along the way, there have been some ideas, methods and products I've found extremely beneficial. In a continuing effort to help other pet sitters and to improve the standards of the pet-sitting industry, I've made many of these items available at reasonable prices through my pet-sitting supply company, Patti Moran's. A list of some of these products follows. They're all tried and true products that will assist you in efficiently, economically and professionally operating your pet-sitting business. A catalog is available that describes these and other products in more detail. Be sure to mention you're a reader of this book because the catalog is free to readers!

- *Professional Pet-Sitting Starter Kit.* Allows you to start pet sitting professionally easily and economically. Available in four versions to meet your career goals.

- *The New Pet Sitter Video.* Forty-five–minute orientation video covers day-to-day basics of responsible pet-sitting care. An all-inclusive resource that comes with a pop quiz. A valuable training aid that allows you to professionally train and test staff members.

- *Business Forms for Pet-Sitting Professionals.* These forms save you valuable time and streamline your office procedures while enhancing your company's image. Everything from the all-important service contract and sitter evaluations to employment applications is available. Each camera-ready form may be reprinted by your local printer.

- What IS Pet Sitting? *Video.* This seven-minute video describes the benefits of leaving a pet at home and explains how most professional pet-sitting services operate. A terrific public relations aid, this video will enhance your guest-speaking engagements and impress viewers with the professionalism of the pet-sitting industry.

- *PZZZ...Ads Advertisement Campaign.* A successful, market-tested ad campaign that brings your service increased revenues and name recognition, while bringing a smile to your customer's face. Seasonal, holiday and year-round ads. Camera-ready material.
- *Pawsitively Proud Professional Pet Sitter Apparel.* T-shirts, sweatshirts, sweatpants and shorts. Comfortable and color-coordinated, this casual attire allows you to look neat, remain comfortable and be prepared for muddy paws!

And there's more! Pet first aid kits and books . . . doorknob hangers . . . pet place mats . . . client reminder cards . . . daily diaries . . . business plan for pet sitters . . . *Selling Your Pet Sitting Business* . . . sitter schedule sheets . . . "survival bags" and pet-sitting "paks" . . . rain ponchos . . . and more! For more information on these and our other products, please write or call:

The Professional Pet Sitters' Best Friend"

Patti Moran's
418 East King Street, Dept. H
King, NC 27021

Orders only: (800) 380-PETS
Fax (orders only): (336) 983-3755
Customer Service: (336) 983-2444

E-mail: petsitin@ols.net
World Wide Web: http://www.petsitproducts.com

PET-RELATED ORGANIZATIONS

The following list contains contact information on organizations that may be of interest to pet-sitting entrepreneurs:

American Animal Hospital Association (AAHA)
12575 West Bayaud Avenue
Lakewood, CO 80228
(303) 986-2800

American Pet Products Manufacturer's Association (APPMA)
255 Glenville Road
Greenwich, CT 06831
(203) 532-0000
Fax: (203) 532-0551

National Foundation of Independent Business (NFIB)
Administrative Office
150 West 20th Avenue
San Mateo, CA 94403
(415) 341-7441

National Foundation for Women Business Owners (NFWBO)
1100 Wayne Avenue, Suite 830
Silver Spring, MD 20910-5603
(301) 495-4975
Fax: (301) 495-4979
E-mail: NFWBO@worldnet.att.net

American Humane Society (AHS)
63 Inverness Drive East
Englewood, CO 80112
(800) 227-4645

The Humane Society of the United States
2100 L Street, NW
Washington, D.C. 20037
(301) 258-3070 or (202) 452-1100
Fax: (301) 258-3074

Pet Sitters International
418 East King Street
King, NC 27021
(336) 983-9222
Nationwide Locator Line: (800) 268-SITS (7487)
(for pet owners wanting to locate a pet sitter)
Fax: (336) 983-3755
E-mail: petsitin@ols.net
WWW: http://www.petsit.com

PSI RECOMMENDATIONS FOR EXCELLENCE IN PET SITTING

Recommended Quality Standards for Excellence in Pet Sitting

- The sitter is bonded and insured.
- The sitter provides references.
- The sitter has experience caring for pets and is clearly mindful of their safety and well-being.
- The sitter provides written literature describing services and stating fees.
- The sitter visits the client's home before the first pet-sitting assignment to meet the pets and get detailed information about their care.
- The sitter shows a positive attitude during the initial meeting and seems comfortable and competent in dealing with animals.
- The sitter wants to learn as much as possible about the animals in his or her care.
- The sitter provides a service contract that specifies services and fees.
- The sitter is courteous, interested and well-informed.
- The sitter keeps regular office hours and answers client inquiries and complaints promptly.
- The sitter takes precautions to make sure a client's absence from home is not detected because of any careless actions or disclosures by the sitter.
- The sitter conducts business with honesty and integrity and observes all federal, state and local laws pertaining to business operations and animal care.
- The sitter has a veterinarian on call for emergency services.
- The sitter has a contingency plan for pet care in case of inclement weather or personal illness.
- The sitting service provides initial and ongoing training for its sitters.
- The sitting service screens applicants for employment carefully.

- The sitter calls to confirm or has the client call to confirm the client has returned home as scheduled.
- The sitter refrains from criticizing competitors.
- The sitter provides a service rating form for clients.
- The sitter exhibits courtesy and professionalism in all dealings with staff members, customers and industry colleagues to present the pet sitter and the pet sitting industry favorably and positively.

POSTSCRIPT

Several years ago, my husband and I purchased a travel book before taking a trip through Europe. We found the book especially helpful, not only for information the author supplied, but also for the tips and suggestions readers had provided from their European travels. In past editions of this book, I told readers that I would like to provide this same kind of firsthand experience from readers in subsequent revisions. As you can see, many useful and interesting tips have, indeed, been supplied by caring—and appreciative—readers. If you learned from any of this shared knowledge, please repay the favor as you learn and grow in professional pet sitting. Please write or e-mail me at Pet Sitters International about things you find helpful and successful in your pet-sitting service. I'll try to incorporate them in future editions.

It's a big world out there with lots of room for successful pet-sitting services. Let's help ourselves, our colleagues and our industry to be the best we can be. I wish you good luck and good fortune with your pet-sitting business!